LOCAL HISTORY

IN

WEST SUSSEX

A GUIDE TO SOURCES

by

KIM C. LESLIE

and

TIMOTHY J. McCANN

Published by

THE WEST SUSSEX COUNTY COUNCIL

COUNTY HALL, CHICHESTER

First published 1971

2nd revised edition 1975

CONTENTS

page

INTRODUCTION   v

PART I   PRINTED SOURCES
             Bibliography   1
             Victoria County History   2
             Other County Histories   2
             Parochial, Manorial and Municipal Histories   3
             Periodic Publications   4
             Select Bibliographies   8
             Directories   24
             Guide Books   25
             Newspapers   25
             Decennial Census Returns   27
             Other Parliamentary Papers   28
             Acts of Parliament   29
             Poll Books   29
             Electoral Registers   30
             Specialist Libraries in the West Sussex Record Office   30
             Unpublished Theses   31

PART II   PICTORIAL AND ORAL SOURCES
             Maps and Plans   35
             Drawings, Prints, Photographs and Postcards   41
             Oral History   43

PART III   DOCUMENTARY SOURCES
             Judicial and Administrative Records   44
             Lieutenancy and Militia Records   45
             Episcopal Records   45
             Capitular Records   47
             Parish Records   47
             Roman Catholic and Nonconformist Records   48
             Borough Records   49
             District Council Records   50
             Poor Law and Welfare Records   50
             Education Records   50
             Highway Records   51
             Railway Records   52
             Land Drainage Records   52
             Inland Navigation Records   53
             Harbour Commissioners and Coastal Shipping Records   53

page

Taxation Records   53

Manorial and Estate Records   54

Miscellaneous Collections in the West Sussex Record
  Office   56

Correspondence Collections in the West Sussex Record
  Office   56

Antiquarian Collections in the West Sussex Record
  Office   58

Collections not in the West Sussex Record Office   59

INTRODUCTION to second edition

The purpose of this booklet is threefold: firstly to provide a list of the main groups of both printed and manuscript source material for the benefit of those unfamiliar with local history research; secondly to furnish brief, but specific, details of some of the material available within each of these groups relevant either to Sussex generally, or to West Sussex in particular; thirdly, to indicate the finding aids in use at the West Sussex County and Diocesan Record Offices, Chichester. The majority of the material listed is available for consultation here, although references to sources located elsewhere have also been included. In this connection it should be emphasised that in West Sussex the most extensive collections of printed books on the county's history are at the Chichester and Worthing Libraries.

In this second edition the opportunity has been taken to extend and update as much of the information as possible, and, in particular, to take into consideration the effects of local government re-organisation in April 1974. By this the county of West Sussex has been enlarged through the transfer of quite a large area from East Sussex. *It should be noted that throughout this booklet the references to West Sussex relate to the new administrative county dating from 1974.* Under re-organisation the following places were added to West Sussex:

Albourne, Ansty, Ardingly, Balcombe, Bolney, Burgess Hill, Clayton, Copthorne, Crawley Down, Cuckfield, Fulking, East Grinstead, Handcross, Hassocks, Haywards Heath, West Hoathly, Horsted Keynes, Hurstpierpoint, Keymer, Lindfield, Newtimber, Poynings, Pycombe, Sayers Common, Scaynes Hill, Slaugham, Staplefield, Turners Hill, Twineham, Warninglid, Worth.

In most cases the records of these places have been transferred from the East Sussex to the West Sussex Record Office, except where this would have meant the breaking up of an archive group, as with the Quarter Sessions records, for example. Where certain classes of records relating to West Sussex have been retained in the East Sussex Record Office this is indicated in Part III of the handbook.

The following are recommended as general introductory guides to the scope and use of county and diocesan record offices:

R. B. Pugh, *How to Write a Parish History* (1954).

F. G. Emmison and Irvine Gray, *County Records* (3rd edn. 1967).

W. E. Tate, *The Parish Chest* (3rd edn. 1969).

David Iredale, *Enjoying Archives* (1973).

W. B. Stephens, *Sources for English local history* (1973).

F. G. Emmison, *Archives and Local History* (2nd edn. 1974).

KIM C. LESLIE
TIMOTHY J. McCANN

PART I   PRINTED SOURCES

BIBLIOGRAPHY

Although no comprehensive bibliography relating to Sussex has yet been published, several attempts have been made:

G. Slade Butler, 'Topographica Sussexiana: an attempt towards forming a list of the various publications relating to the County of Sussex' in *Sussex Archaeological Collections*, vol. 15 (1863), pp. 215–230; vol. 16 (1864), pp. 273–290; vol. 17 (1865), pp. 169–184; vol. 18 (1866), pp. 87–110. The bibliography was reprinted and published as a separate volume in 1866.

Frederick Ernest Sawyer, 'Recent Sussex Bibliography (1864–1881)' in *Sussex Archaeological Collections*, vol. 32 (1882), pp. 201–212. Vol. 33 (1883), pp. 207–212, adds books published in 1882, and an addendum for 1864–1881.

Irene Hernaman, 'A List of Sussex Books' in *Sussex County Magazine*, vol. 4 (1930), pp. 69–73; 158–164; followed by a supplementary list, pp. 1027–1028.

Eliot Curwen, 'Bibliographical Index to archaeological matter relating to Sussex appearing elsewhere than in the publications of the Sussex Archaeological Society' in the *General Index to Sussex Archaeological Collections, vols. 51–75 and Sussex Notes and Queries, vols. 1–4* (1936), pp. 487–522. A supplement by Curwen and W. H. Godfrey was published in the *Sussex Archaeological Collections*, vol. 82 (1942), pp. 141–152. The term 'archaeology' is used to cover a wide variety of historical matters.

Eastbourne Public Library published a *Catalogue of the Local Collection comprising books on Eastbourne and Sussex* (1956), compiled by C. L. Pinnock. This includes many books published before 1936 which were not listed in Curwen's index and provides a bibliography to 1955.

John Farrant's 'Sussex Bibliography' for 1970, 1971, and 1972, published in the *Sussex Archaeological Society Newsletter* (no. 3, Sept. 1971; no. 7, Sept. 1972; no. 11, Sept. 1973, respectively) records books, pamphlets and articles relating to the county published in these three years. The 1973 bibliography has been published in 1975 as *Sussex Archaeological Society Occasional Paper No. 3*. The 1974 bibliography has been published in 1975 by the East Sussex County Library Service, Lewes. The East Sussex Library Service has undertaken to publish these annual bibliographies in the future.

The first two publications in a new series of Occasional Papers by the University of Sussex Centre for Continuing Education are select bibliographies prepared principally for those intending to teach Sussex local history to adult classes. These are invaluable, none the less, to the student and scholar:

John Farrant, *Sussex in the 18th and 19th Centuries: A Bibliography* (1973).

Colin E. Brent, Anthony J. Fletcher and Timothy J. McCann, *Sussex in the 16th and 17th Centuries: A Bibliography* (1974).

A further bibliography, on medieval Sussex, is in preparation.

The principal printed sources relating to the history of Sussex listed below are available for consultation at the several reference libraries in the county, and in both the East and West Sussex Record Offices. The key letters given in brackets in the following list are used to indicate their location in the libraries at:

Bognor (B); Brighton (BN); Burgess Hill (BH); Chichester (CHI); Crawley (C); East Grinstead (EG); East Sussex County Library Headquarters, Lewes (ESX); East Sussex Record Office, Lewes (ESRO); Haywards Heath (HH); Horsham (H); Hove (HV); Lancing (L); Littlehampton (LN); Midhurst (M); Petworth (P); Shoreham-by-Sea (S); Southwick (SK); Sussex Archaeological Society, Lewes (SAS); West Sussex Record Office, Chichester (WSRO); Worthing (W).

VICTORIA COUNTY HISTORY (B; BN; BH; CHI; C; EG; ESX; ESRO; HH; H; HV; L; LN; M; P; S; SK; SAS; WSRO; W.)

The Sussex volumes form part of a national survey which commenced publication in 1900. The aim has been to describe the history of every English county on a uniform basis, written from original sources to replace the older county histories. The first two Sussex volumes contain general themes: volume 1 covers natural history, geology, early man, Anglo-Saxon remains, the Domesday Survey, earthworks and political history; volume 2, ecclesiastical history, religious houses (with a detailed account of the Dissolution), maritime, social and economic history, population statistics 1801–1901, industries (iron, bell-founding, pottery, brickmaking, glass, textiles, tanning, brewing, cider-making, fisheries), agriculture, forestry, architecture, schools and sport; volume 3 is a study of Romano-British Sussex and the history of the City of Chichester. Subsequent volumes are topographical, being accounts of each parish arranged by hundreds. Normally each parochial description includes geographical features and communications, manorial descent, the church, advowson, charities and principal buildings. Volumes 4, 7 and 9 cover the Rapes of Chichester, Lewes and Hastings respectively. Work is at present in progress on a volume to cover the southern half of the Rape of Bramber (including Worthing), to be followed by a separate volume on the northern half (including Horsham). In these volumes the parochial descriptions will have a much wider scope than hitherto, with more emphasis on landscape and social and economic history. Volumes on the Rapes of Arundel and Pevensey, and an index to the complete series, have yet to be started.

A *General Introduction* giving the origin and progress of the Victoria County History, listing the contents of the first 150 volumes, with indexes of the titles of articles and of authors, was published in 1970.

The Sussex volumes are now available in facsimile from Dawsons of Pall Mall, Cannon House, Folkestone, Kent.

OTHER COUNTY HISTORIES

The emphasis of these earlier county histories is on political, manorial and ecclesiastical history. In many parts those by Dallaway and Cartwright, and Horsfield, are somewhat hasty and careless compilations, and should be used with caution.

J. Dallaway and E. Cartwright, *A History of the Western Division of the County of Sussex*. Volume 1, general historical introduction to the county, and City and Rape of Chichester (1815); volume 2, part I, Rape of Arundel (1819; 2nd edn. 1832); part II, Rape of Bramber (1830). (BN; CHI; C; ESX; H; HV; S; SAS; WSRO; W.)

For a biographical account of James Dallaway, and his compilation of this history, see Francis W. Steer, 'Memoir and Letters of James Dallaway, 1763–1834' in *Sussex Archaeological Collections*, vol. 103 (1965), pp. 1–48; for a postscript to this article see vol. 105 (1967), pp. 62–69.

Thomas Walker Horsfield, *The History, Antiquities and Topography of the County of Sussex* (1835). Volume 1, general historical introduction and a contemporary survey of the county, Rapes of Lewes, Pevensey and Hastings; volume 2, Rapes of Chichester, Arundel and Bramber, Appendix of climate, botany, parliamentary history, ecclesiastical divisions and general statistical tables.

Both volumes have been re-published in facsimile by Kohler & Coombes of Dorking in 1974, with an introductory article by Francis W. Steer. (B; BN; BH; CHI; C; EG; ESX; ESRO; HH; H; HV; L; LN; M; P; S; SK; SAS; WSRO; W.)

M. A. Lower, *A Compendious History of Sussex, topographical, archaeological and anecdotical* (1870). Volume 1 gives a very brief survey of the county's history, industry and geology, and parochial descriptions, Adversane to Itchingfield; volume 2, Jevington to Yapton. (B; BN; CHI; C; EG; ESX; ESRO; H; HV; L; S; SAS; WSRO; W.)

J. R. Armstrong, *A History of Sussex* (3rd edn. 1974). The best and most comprehensive introduction to the history of the county, from geological to modern times. (B; BN; BH; CHI; C; EG; ESX; ESRO; HH; H; HV; L; LN; M; P; S; SK; SAS; WSRO; W.)

PAROCHIAL, MANORIAL AND MUNICIPAL HISTORIES

These vary in reliability. Whilst many published this century have been pre-occupied with manorial, ecclesiastical and general antiquarian themes, a number can be recommended for both well-balanced scope and accuracy. Some of the best in this category are:

J. H. Cooper, *A History of the Parish of Cuckfield* (1912).

G. W. Eustace, *Arundel: Borough and Castle* (1922).

William Albery, *A Millennium of Facts in the History of Horsham and Sussex 947–1947* (1947).

Lindsay Fleming, *History of Pagham in Sussex*, 3 vols. (1949–50).

Lord Leconfield, *Petworth Manor in the Seventeenth Century* (1954).

The most detailed published survey of a Regency/Victorian town in West Sussex is for Worthing, in a series of books issued by the Worthing Art Development Scheme between 1938 and 1954. Much of their value is in the finely-executed publication of a wealth of formerly unpublished or little-known reminiscences and early photographs. Central to the series are:

Edward Snewin and Henfrey Smail, *Glimpses of Old Worthing* (1945).

Henfrey Smail, *The Worthing Map Story* (1949).

Possibly the best study of a particular district is

E. Heron-Allen, *Selsey Bill: historic and prehistoric* (1911).

Printed works relating to West Sussex towns are listed below (pp. 21–23). Village and parish histories will be located by reference to the bibliographies listed above (p. 1), and to catalogue entries in the various libraries in the county, and the East and West Sussex Record Offices at Lewes and Chichester.

MONOGRAPHS

Three series of monographs are published: the *Chichester Papers*, the *Harting Papers*, and the *Littlehampton Papers*. A selection is noted in the subject bibliographies, pp. 8–23.

CHURCH GUIDES

Comprehensive collections of guides to West Sussex churches are held at Chichester and Worthing Libraries and the West Sussex Record Office. Many churches have been described in a series of uniform official Diocese of Chichester guides prepared by Walter H. Godfrey and Francis W. Steer.

PERIODIC PUBLICATIONS

The following sets of publications are incomplete at several of the county libraries. Where this is so the key letter is marked *inc.*

A Sussex Archaeological Society publications

i *Sussex Archaeological Collections*. (B; BN; BH *inc*; CHI; C *inc*; EG; ESX; ESRO; HH *inc*; H; HV; L *inc*; LN; M *inc*; P *inc*; S; SK; SAS; WSRO; W.)

The Society's annual transactions first published in 1848. Records the results of research on the archaeology, architecture and history of the county, and the business of the Society. Volumes indexed individually, also composite indexes every 25 volumes. A comprehensive index of authors and articles for volumes 1–111 (1848–1974), indexed by persons, places and subjects, is to be published shortly by the West Sussex Record Office.

ii *Sussex Notes and Queries* (B *inc*; BN; BH *inc*; CHI; C *inc*; EG *inc*; ESX; ESRO; H *inc*; HV; L *inc*; S *inc*; SAS; WSRO; W.)

This quarterly, later half-yearly, journal of the Society, published between 1926 and 1971, includes brief notes, short articles and requests for information. A general index to the series is incorporated in the index volumes of the *Collections*.

iii *Occasional Papers* (B; BN; CHI; C; ESX; ESRO; H; HV; L; M *inc*; S; SAS; WSRO; W.)

A venture commenced in 1970 for publishing papers considered too long for inclusion in the *Collections*.

iv *Newsletter* (B; BN; CHI; C; ESX; ESRO; H; HV; L; S; SAS; WSRO; W.)

First published in 1970 (half-yearly until March 1972, thereafter quarterly) as an aid to study and research. Includes coverage of forthcoming events, excavations, classes and lectures, exhibitions, work in progress, requests for information and assistance, accessions to the East and West Sussex Record Offices, and an annual bibliography of Sussex books. (This bibliographical service has been discontinued in the *Newsletter*, see p. 1.)

B Sussex Record Society publications (B *inc*; BN; BH *inc*; CHI; C *inc*; EG *inc*; ESX; ESRO; H *inc*; HV; S *inc*; SAS; WSRO; W.)

Founded for the publication of records and documents relating to the county, the Society has issued annual volumes since 1902. Publications include marriage licences, fines, post-mortem inquisitions, ecclesiastical returns, parish registers, manorial records, apprenticeship indentures, chantry records, wills, gamekeepers' deputations, quarter sessions records, Star Chamber proceedings, etc. A selection of particular West Sussex relevance is:

volume

1 *Calendar of Sussex Marriage Licences . . . Archdeaconry of Lewes, August, 1586, to March 1642–3* (1902).

5 *West Sussex Protestation Returns, 1641–2* (1906).

6 *Calendar of Sussex Marriage Licences . . . Archdeaconry of Lewes, August, 1670, to March, 1728–9, and . . . Deanery of South Malling, May, 1620, to December, 1732* (1907).

8/11 *The Episcopal Register of Robert Rede . . . Lord Bishop of Chichester, 1397–1415* (1908, 1910).

9 *Calendar of Sussex Marriage Licences . . . Archdeaconry of Chichester, June, 1575, to December, 1730* (1909).

12 *Calendar of Sussex Marriage Licences . . . Deanery of Chichester, January, 1582–3, to December, 1730, and Deaneries of Pagham and Tarring, January, 1579–80, to November, 1730* (1911).

13 *The Parish Registers of Cuckfield, Sussex, 1598–1699* (1911).

15 *The Parish Registers of Bolney, Sussex, 1541–1812* (1912).

17 *The Parish Registers of Ardingly, Sussex, 1558–1812* (1913).

18 *The First Book of the Parish Registers of Angmering, Sussex, 1562–1687* (1913).

21 *The Parish Register of Horsham in the County of Sussex, 1541–1635* (1915).

22 *The Parish Register of Cowfold, Sussex, 1558–1812* (1916).

24 *The Parish Register of East Grinstead, Sussex, 1558–1661* (1917).

25/26 *Calendar of Sussex Marriage Licences . . . Archdeaconry of Lewes and . . . Deanery of South Malling, 1772–1837* (1917, 1919).

31 *Thirteen Custumals of the Sussex Manors of the Bishop of Chichester* (1925). Includes Aldingbourne, Amberley, Cakeham, Drungewick, Ferring, Rackham, Selsey, Sidlesham and Stretham.

32 *Calendar of Sussex Marriage Licences . . . Archdeaconry of Chichester, January, 1731, to December, 1774* (1926).

34 *The Book of John Rowe, Steward of the Manors of Lord Bergavenny, 1597–1622* (1928). Includes West Chiltington, Cuckfield, Keymer and Nutbourne.

35   *Calendar of Sussex Marriage Licences . . . Archdeaconry of Chichester, January, 1775, to December, 1800* (1929).

39   *The Buckhurst Terrier, 1597–1598* (1933). Includes land in East Grinstead.

41/42/ *Transcripts of Sussex Wills* (1935, 1937, 1938, 1941). The four vol-
43/45 umes relate to the following parishes respectively; Albourne to Chichester; Chiddingly to Horsham; Horsted Keynes to Pyecombe; Racton to Yapton.

44   *Records of the Baronry and Honour of the Rape of Lewes* (1940).

46   *The Chartulary of the High Church of Chichester* (1946).

49/50 *Churchwardens' Presentments (17th century): Part 1, Archdeaconry of Chichester . . . Part 2, Archdeaconry of Lewes* (1948, 1949).

52   *The Acts of the Dean and Chapter of the Cathedral Church of Chichester, 1472–1544* (1952).

55   *Ministers' Accounts of the Manor of Petworth, 1347–1353* (1955).

57   *Custumals of the Sussex Manors of the Archbishop of Canterbury* (1958). Includes Lavant, Malling, Slindon, Tangmere and Tarring.

58   *The Acts of the Dean and Chapter of the Cathedral Church of Chichester, 1545–1642* (1959).

59   *The Chartulary of Boxgrove Priory* (1960).

60   *Custumals of the Manors of Laughton, Willingdon and Goring* (1961).

62   *Minute Book of the Common Council of the City of Chichester, 1783–1826* (1963).

67   *Two Estate Surveys of the Fitzalan Earls of Arundel* (1969).

68   *The Journal of Giles Moore* (1971). Rector of Horsted Keynes in the 17th century.

C Sussex County Magazine (B; BN; BH *inc*; CHI; C; EG; ESX; ESRO; HH *inc*; H; HV; L *inc*; LN; M *inc*; P *inc*; S; SAS; WSRO; W.)

Profusely illustrated monthly journal published between 1926 and 1956 to record the archaeology, history and folk-lore of the county. Many of the articles are of a good standard representing original research. An accompanying index volume was published by Hove Public Library in 1966. A more detailed card index to the complete set is held by Chichester Library.

D Sussex Industrial History (B; BN; BH *inc*; CHI; C; ESX; ESRO; HH *inc*; H; HV; L; M *inc*; S; SAS; WSRO; W.)

Half-yearly journal of industrial archaeology and history, published between winter 1970–1 and winter 1973–4, in six issues, since discontinued. The articles with information relating to West Sussex include: D. F. Gibbs and J. H. Farrant, 'The Upper Ouse Navigation, 1790–1868' (no. 1, 1970–1).

Michael Worthington-Williams, 'Dolphin Motors of Shoreham' (no. 2, 1971).

Margaret Holt, 'Lime Kilns in Central Sussex' (no. 2, 1971).

Adrian Barritt, 'Kingston Malthouse, 1844–1971' (no. 3, 1971–2).

John H. Farrant, 'A Bridge for Littlehampton, 1821–22' (no. 5, 1972–3).

John H. Farrant, 'Civil Engineering in Sussex around 1800, and the Career of Cater Rand' (no. 6, 1973–4).

John Hoare, 'Railway Architecture in Sussex' (no. 6, 1973–4).

John A. Bagley, 'Shoreham and Ford: A History of two Sussex Airfields' (no. 6, 1973–4).

E Sussex Life (B; BN; BH *inc*; CHI; C; EG *inc*; ESX; HH *inc*; H; HV; L *inc*; LN; M; S; SK; SAS; W.)

Monthly magazine first published May 1965, covering a wide range of county activities, with many articles of a historic nature. Several of these articles contain useful material not found elsewhere, and they are usually well illustrated. An index to the first ten years is in active preparation (1975).

F Sussex Family Historian (BN; CHI; C *inc*; ESX; ESRO; HV; S; SAS; WSRO; W.)

Quarterly journal of the Sussex Family History Group, first published June 1973, with genealogical articles based on original research, advice on the use of documents, transcripts, work in progress and members' queries, etc.

G Wealden Iron (CHI *inc*; C *inc*; EG *inc*; ESX; ESRO *inc*; HH *inc*; HV *inc*; SAS; WSRO *inc*; W *inc*.)

Bulletin of the Wealden Iron Research Group, first published 1971 (undated), with articles relating to current research into the local iron industry.

H The Gentleman's Magazine

BN   1731–1860; 1868–74; 1877–78.

CHI   1731–1843.

SAS   1731–58; 1760–80; 1784–89; 1791–1845; 1847–48; 1850–54; 1871–87; 1889.

WSRO   1754–80; 1794–95; 1797–1808; 1812–29.

Monthly magazine published between 1731 and 1907 with articles on domestic and foreign news, the weather, prices, etc., and correspondence, book reviews, obituaries and short essays on antiquarian, historical, literary, scientific and topographical subjects, etc. For the local historian there is much useful information of a social and topographical nature. For references and transcripts of the topographical descriptions relating to Sussex see F. A. Milne (ed.), *The Gentleman's Magazine Library: being a classified collection of the chief contents of the Gentleman's Magazine from 1731 to 1868: English Topography, Part XII (Surrey-Sussex)* (1900).

I The Annual Register

BN   1758 to date.

CHI   1758–1831; 1833–34; 1913; 1924–26; 1929–30; 1933–35; 1937; 1940–41; 1945 to date.

HV   1758 to date.
WSRO   1758–1839; 1863–1900; 1906–10; 1916; 1918.
W   1922; 1933; 1947; 1949; 1965 to date.

Annual record, published from 1758 to date, of domestic and foreign affairs in politics, economics, science, religion and the arts, obituaries of eminent persons, etc. There are some useful references for the local historian, especially in the earlier volumes, and the series, as a whole, provides a valuable contemporaiy framework of national and international events.

SELECT BIBLIOGRAPHIES

It is emphasised that the following lists are selective. For some of the subjects there are cross references to two recently published bibliographies: John Farrant, *Sussex in the 18th and 19th Centuries: A Bibliography* (1973), and Colin E. Brent, Anthony J. Fletcher and Timothy J. McCann, *Sussex in the 16th and 17th Centuries: A Bibliography* (1974).

AGRICULTURE

See also Geology and the Land, and also Countryside and Folklore.

Farrant, pp. 28–29; Brent, Fletcher, McCann, pp. 16–20.

Rev. Arthur Young, *General View of the Agriculture of the County of Sussex* (1793). A much enlarged 2nd edition was published in 1808, and re-issued in 1813. The 1813 impression has been published in facsimile (1970), by David & Charles.

Edmund Scott, *Proceedings of the Sussex Agricultural Society from its institution to 1798* (1800).

William Marshall, *The Review and Abstract of the County Reports to the Board of Agriculture; from the several Agricultural Departments of England*, vol. 5 (1817, re-issued 1818). The Sussex section comprises a short introduction, and a commentary on, and synopsis of, Arthur Young's 2nd edition (see above). The 1818 impression has been reprinted in facsimile (1969), by David & Charles.

The Domesday Book for the County of Sussex . . . 1873 . . . (1876). Return of land-holding in Sussex, made in 1873 (sometimes known as the Second Domesday), with the names of owners of land of one acre and upwards, the estimated acreage and annual gross estimated rental of each property. Prefaced by introductory notes.

W. D. Parish (ed.), *Domesday Book in relation to the County of Sussex* (1886). Facsimile of the original text of the first great Domesday Survey made in the 11th century, with an extended transcription and translation of the Latin text, and an introduction.

Charles Reginald Haines, *A Complete Memoir of Richard Haines (1633–1685)* (1899). A yeoman farmer of Sullington, involved also in fruit farming and cider-making.

H. Rider Haggard, *Rural England*, vol. 1 (1902). An account of agricultural and social researches carried out in 1901 and 1902, with a chapter relating to Sussex.

A. D. Hall and E. J. Russell, *Agriculture and Soils of Kent, Surrey and Sussex* (1911).

8

E. Walford Lloyd, *The Southdown Sheep* (1933).

E. Walford Lloyd, *Sussex Cattle* (*c.* 1945).

W. E. Tate, *A Handlist of Sussex Inclosure Acts and Awards* (1950). Reprinted from *Sussex Archaeological Collections*, vol. 88 (1949), pp. 114–156.

R. H. B. Jesse, *A Survey of the Agriculture of Sussex* (1960).

Ronald Webber, *Market Gardening: The History of Commercial Flower, Fruit and Vegetable Growing* (1972). Brief references to market gardening on the West Sussex coastal plain, especially at Worthing.

ARCHITECTURE, INCLUDING CHURCH FABRIC

Note: the best and most comprehensive introduction to all aspects of architecture in the county is Ian Nairn and Nikolaus Pevsner, *The Buildings of England: Sussex* (1965).

Domestic: vernacular

E. Guy Dawber, *Old Cottages and Farmhouses in Kent and Sussex* (1900).

Viscountess Wolseley, *Some of the Smaller Manor Houses of Sussex* (1925).

Valentine Fletcher, *Chimney Pots and Stacks* (1968). Includes a number of Sussex items, especially in Chichester.

R. T. Mason, *Framed Buildings of the Weald* (2nd edn. 1969).

E. M. Venables and A. F. Outen, *Building Stones of Old Bognor* (1969). Bognor Regis Natural Science Society publication no. 3.

H. M. and U. E. Lacy, *The Timber-Framed Buildings of Steyning* (1974).

Domestic: the larger houses

William Hayley Mason, *Goodwood, its House, Park and Grounds* (1839).

Mrs. Charles Roundell, *Cowdray: The History of a Great English House* (1884).

Gerald W. E. Loder, *Wakehurst Place, Sussex* (1907).

W. H. St. John Hope, *Cowdray and Easebourne Priory* (1919).

Christopher Hussey, *Petworth House, Sussex* (1926).

[James Wentworth-Fitzwilliam], *Parham in Sussex* (1947).

Notable Houses of Worthing series published by the Worthing Art Development Scheme:

Anon., *1: Beach House* (1947).

Henfrey Smail, *2: Offington, Broadwater Manor, Charmandean* (1950).

Henfrey Smail, *5: Warwick House* (1952).

Henfrey Smail, *6: Courtlands* (1952).

Antony Dale, *James Wyatt* (1956). Refers to his Sussex commissions, including the Assembly Rooms, Chichester; Goodwood; Petworth Prison (or House of Correction); Stansted; West Dean.

Earl of Bessborough, *A Place in the Forest: Being the story of Stansted in Sussex* (1958).

Margaret Meade-Fetherstonhaugh and Oliver Warner, *Uppark and its People* (1964).

Church architecture

R. Willis, J. L. Petit and E. Sharpe, *The Architectural History of Chichester Cathedral, Boxgrove Priory and Shoreham Collegiate Church* (1861).

R. H. Nibbs and Mark Antony Lower, *The Churches of Sussex* (1872).

A. H. Peat and L. C. Halstead, *Churches and other Antiquities of West Sussex* (1912).

Frederick Harrison, *Notes on Sussex Churches* (4th edn. 1920).

Francis W. Steer, *The Church of St. John the Evangelist, Chichester, 1813–1963* (Chichester Paper no. 35, 1963).

Francis W. Steer (ed.), *Chichester Cathedral Essays* (1965). Reprint of ten titles from the Chichester Papers series.

John L. Denman, *A Survey of the Structural Development of Sussex Churches* (1967).

E. A. Fisher, *Saxon Churches of Sussex* (1970).

M. C. W. Hunter, *The Restorations of Harting Church, 1796–1876* (1970). Harting Paper no. 1.

Francis W. Steer, *The Cathedral Church of Our Lady and Saint Philip, Arundel* (1973).

[Walter Hussey, ed.], *Chichester 900* (1975). Commemorating the nine hundredth anniversary of the foundation of the Cathedral.

Alison McCann, *Chichester Cathedral; a brief history* (1975). Commentary accompanying *Prints from the Past Set 3: Chichester Cathedral* (reproductions of four prints), published by the Archives and Library Services of the West Sussex County Council.

Church fabric

T. C. Woodman, *The Sussex Brasses* (1903). In two parts.

H. R. Mosse, *The Monumental Effigies of Sussex, 1250–1650* (2nd edn. 1933).

M. F. Drummond Roberts, *Some Sussex fonts photographed and described* (1935).

Anon., *The Treasures of the Sussex Churches* (1937).

Clive Bell, *Twelfth Century Paintings at Hardham and Clayton* (1947).

George P. Elphick, *Sussex Bells and Belfries* (1970).

Railway architecture

Nigel Wikeley and John Middleton, *Railway Stations: Southern Region* (1971).

Rodney Symes and David Cole, *Railway Architecture of the South-East* (1972).

John Hoare, 'Railway Architecture in Sussex' in *Sussex Industrial History*, no. 6 (Winter 1973–4), pp. 15–24.

COUNTRYSIDE AND FOLKLORE

See also Agriculture and also Reminiscences

The Sussex countryside has been effusively described in scores of books, a great many of which rely more on exaggerated romance and quaintness than reality. However, the few written by genuine countrymen are worthwhile for the local historian and those trying to understand character and traditional patterns of country life in the past. Some of the following titles relate to East Sussex.

William Cobbett, *Cottage Economy* (1821). Republished (1926) by Peter Davies. Instructions in domestic management for the labouring classes, including brewing beer, keeping animals, making bread, rush lights, straw hats, and ice houses. Much of the information was gathered from Sussex, whilst Cobbett was staying at Worth.

Charlotte Latham, 'Some West Sussex Superstitions Lingering in 1868' in *The Folk-Lore Record*, part 1 (1878), pp. 7–61.

Raymond Jacberns (ed.), *Southward Ho! A Sussex Monthly Magazine of Fact, Fiction and Verse* (December 1893–July 1895). This short-lived magazine is noteworthy for its articles on folklore, legends, and dialect.

John Halsham [George Forrester Scott], *Idlehurst: A Journal Kept in the Country* (1898). Changes in mid-Sussex during the late Victorian period. *Idlehurst*, the author's home in *Arnington*, is the Manor house in Lindfield.

Arthur Beckett, *The Spirit of the Downs* (1909).

Arthur Beckett, *The Wonderful Weald* (1911).

Tickner Edwardes, *Neighbourhood: A Year's Life in and about an English Village* (1911). *Windlecombe* is Burpham.

Adelaide L. J. Gosset, *Shepherds of Britain* (1911).

Rev. Edward Boys Ellman, *Recollections of a Sussex Parson* (1912). By the rector of Berwick, 1846–1906.

Nathaniel Paine Blaker, *Sussex in Bygone Days* (1919).

Rev. John Coker Egerton, *Sussex Folk and Sussex Ways* (3rd edn. 1924). By the rector of Burwash, 1867–88.

Barclay Wills, *Bypaths in Downland* (1927).

Barclay Wills, *Downland Treasure* (1929).

Barclay Wills, *Shepherds of Sussex* (n.d.).

Amy Sawyer, *Sussex Village Plays* (1934).

H. J. Massingham, *English Downland* (1936).

Maude Robinson, *A South Down Farm in the Sixties* (1938). Nineteenth-century reminiscences of farming at Sadlescombe, Poynings.

William Wood, *A Sussex Farmer* (1938).

Esther Meynell, *Country Ways* (1942).

Esther Meynell, *Small Talk in Sussex* (1954).

Doreen Valiente, *Where Witchcraft Lives* (1962). Concentrates on Sussex.

Francis W. Steer (ed.), *The Memoirs of Gaius Carley, a Sussex Black-Smith* (2nd edn. 1964).

Mavis Budd, *Dust to Dust* (1966)
Mavis Budd, *A Prospect of Love* (1968)
Mavis Budd, *Fit for a Duchess* (1970)

} Cottage and country life near Midhurst in the 1930s, evoking more the flavour of the nineteenth century.

Bob Copper, *A Song for Every Season: A Hundred Years of a Sussex Farming Family* (1971).

John Lowerson, *Victorian Sussex* (1972).

Patricia Squires, *The Ghost in the Mirror* (1972). Sussex ghost stories.

Bob Copper, *Songs and Southern Breezes* (1973). Part is devoted to folk songs collected in Sussex and Hampshire.

Jacqueline Simpson, *The Folklore of Sussex* (1973).

Jacqueline Simpson, 'Sussex Local Legends' in *Folklore*, vol. 84 (Autumn 1973), pp. 206–223.

Maude Egerton King (ed.), *A Cottage Wife's Calendar* (1975). The country year written by the wife of a Harting farm labourer just over fifty years ago, with introductory notes, reprinted by the Harting Society.

Bernard Price, *Sussex: People; Places; Things* (1975).

CULTURE AND LEISURE

Except for the theatre, the whole subject of culture and leisure in Sussex has been little researched, but see also under Countryside and Folklore, Education, and Sport, in this bibliography. Note, however, the forthcoming study by John Lowerson and John Myerscough, *The Dream of Leisure in Victorian Sussex.*

Mary Theresa Odell, *The Old Theatre, Worthing* (1938). The history of the Theatre Royal, Worthing, 1807–55.

Mary Theresa Odell, *More About the Old Theatre, Worthing* (1945). Also includes references to theatrical performances at Arundel, Brighton, Chichester, Horsham, Littlehampton, Petworth and Shoreham.

Mary Theresa Odell, *Some Playbills of the Old Theatre, Worthing* (1955).

Francis W. Steer, *The Chichester Theatre* (Chichester Paper no. 9, 1957). Erected in South Street, Chichester, in 1791.

Francis W. Steer, 'Sources of Information on 18th and Early 19th Century Theatres in Sussex' in *Theatre Notebook*, vol. 12, no. 2 (Winter 1958), pp. 58–64.

Leslie Evershed-Martin, *The Impossible Theatre* (1971). Chichester Festival Theatre which opened in 1962.

DIALECT

William Durrant Cooper, *A Glossary of the Provincialisms in use in the County of Sussex* (2nd edn. 1853).

W. D. Parish, *A Dictionary of the Sussex Dialect and Collection of Provincialisms in use in the County of Sussex* (1875).

Amy Sawyer, *Sussex Village Plays* (1934).

Margaret Wyndham, *Mrs. Paddick* (1947). A series of true village stories in Sussex dialect by Miss L. F. Ramsey of West Wittering writing under a pen name. Note that Miss Ramsey's Mrs. Paddick column of Sussex dialect has been appearing regularly in the *West Sussex Gazette* since 1936. Despite her death in 1974 this feature has been continued by reprinting earlier articles.

Sven Rubin, *The Phonology of the Middle English Dialect of Sussex* (1951). Lund Studies in English, no. 21.

Helena Hall, *A Dictionary of the Sussex Dialect and Collection of Provincialisms in use in the County of Sussex by the Rev. W. D. Parish . . . Expanded, Augmented and Illustrated* (1957).

Harold Orton and Martyn F. Wakelin, *Survey of English Dialects, Volume IV, part 1: The Southern Counties* (1967).

EDUCATION

Farrant, pp. 41–42; Brent, Fletcher, McCann, pp. 33–34.

E. H. Pearce, *Annals of Christ's Hospital* (2nd edn. 1908). Christ's Hospital, or the Bluecoat School, moved from Newgate Street, London, to a site near Horsham in 1902.

Ernest F. Row, *A History of Midhurst Grammar School* (1913).

Edmund Blunden, *Christ's Hospital: A Retrospect* [1923].

Sir John Otter, *Nathaniel Woodard: A Memoir of His Life* (1925). In Sussex, Woodard founded the public schools of Ardingly, Hurstpierpoint and Lancing.

[B. W. T. Handford], *Lancing: A History of SS. Mary and Nicolas College, Lancing, 1848–1930* (1933).

G. A. T. Allan, *Christ's Hospital* (1937).

K. E. Kirk, *The Story of the Woodard Schools* (1937).

R. Perry, *Ardingly, 1858–1946: A History of the School* (1951).

Helena Hall, *William Allen, 1770–1843* (1953). Founder of the Lindfield Schools of Industry (1825–81) as part of an allotment colony for the poor.

C. Burton Fairbrother, *The Oliver Whitby School at Chichester in the County of Sussex, 1702–1950* (1956).

Grace Hine, *The Lancastrian School for Girls, Chichester, 1812–1962* (Chichester Paper no. 26, 1962).

Francis W. Steer, *The Chichester Literary and Philosophical Society and Mechanics' Institute, 1831–1924* (Chichester Paper no. 29, 1962).

A. N. Willson, *History of Collyer's School, 1532–1964* (1965). Horsham.

J. Sleight and G. A. Cockman, *Steyning Grammar School: A History* [1975].

GEOLOGY AND THE LAND

See also Agriculture.

Farrant, pp. 28–29; Brent, Fletcher, McCann, pp. 16–20.

Gideon Mantell, *The Fossils of the South Downs; or Illustrations of the Geology of Sussex* (1822).

Gideon Mantell, *The Geology of the South-East of England* (1833).

Frederick Dixon, *The Geology and Fossils of the Tertiary and Cretaceous Formations of Sussex* (1850).

W. Topley, *The Geology of the Weald* (1875).

William Whitaker and Clement Reid, *The Water Supply of Sussex from Underground Sources* (1899).

William Whitaker, H. R. Mill and H. F. Parsons, *The Water Supply of Sussex from Underground Sources: Supplement* (1911).

Edward A. Martin, *Dew-Ponds, Observation and Experiment* [1915].

Sidney Spokes, *Gideon Algernon Mantell* (1927). Life of the county's pioneer geologist.

F. H. Edmunds, *Wells and Springs of Sussex* (1928).

Arthur H. Schofield, *The West Sussex Coast and Downs* (1929). Report of the Arundel, Littlehampton, East Preston and District Joint Town Planning Advisory Committee.

A. Hadrian Allcroft, *Waters of Arun* (1930). Study of the changing course of the River Arun.

Edward A. Martin, *Outlines of Sussex Geology* (1932).

W. Harding Thompson and Geoffrey Clark, *The Sussex Landscape* (1935).

Alfred A. Pugsley, *Dewponds in Fable and Fact* (1938).

E. Cecil Curwen (ed.), *The Journal of Gideon Mantell* (1940). Journal of the Sussex surgeon and geologist covering the years 1818 to 1852. Records Mantell's pioneer geological excursions in Sussex.

E. W. H. Briault, *The Land of Britain: Sussex* (1942). Parts 83 and 84 of the Report of the Land Utilisation Survey of Britain.

S. W. Wooldridge and Frederick Goldring, *The Weald* (1953).

S. W. Wooldridge and D. L. Linton, *Structure, Surface and Drainage in South-East England* (1955).

H. C. Darby and Eila M. J. Campbell, *The Domesday Geography of South-East England* (1962).

F. H. Edmunds and R. W. Gallois, *The Wealden District* (4th edn. 1965).

J. M. Hodgson, *Soils of the West Sussex Coastal Plain* (1967).

J. M. Hodgson, J. A. Catt and A. H. Weir, *The Origin and Development of Clay-with-Flints and Associated Soil Horizons on the South Downs* (1967).

K. D. Fines, 'Landscape Evaluation: A Research Project in East Sussex' in *Regional Studies*, vol. 2 (1968), pp. 41–55.

R. B. G. Williams (ed.), *Guide to Sussex Excursions* (1971). Handbook to accompany excursions arranged by the Institute of British Geographers' Conference at the University of Sussex, 1971. Includes studies on settlement, geomorphology, land use, recreational and planning problems.

G. S. Burrows, *Landscape Appraisal of West Sussex* (1972). West Sussex County Council Planning Department.

E. M. Yates, *A history of the landscapes of the parishes of South Harting and Rogate* (1972). Harting Paper no. 3.

Peter Brandon, *The Sussex Landscape* (1974).

S. A. Searle, *The Tidal Threat: East Head Spit, Chichester Harbour* (1975).

PLACE NAMES

R. G. Roberts, *The Place Names of Sussex* (1914).

A. Mawer and F. M. Stenton, *The Place Names of Sussex: Part I, the Rapes of Chichester, Arundel and Bramber* (1929). *Part II, the Rapes of Lewes, Pevensey and Hastings* (1930).

E. Ekwall, *The Concise Oxford Dictionary of English Place Names* (1951).

POLITICAL

Farrant, pp. 42–43; Brent, Fletcher, McCann, pp. 35–39.

Anon., *An Entire and Complete History . . . of the Boroughs of Great Britain*, vol. 3 (1792). Includes Arundel, Bramber, Chichester, East Grinstead, Horsham, Midhurst, Shoreham, Steyning.

Simon Fraser, *Reports of the Proceedings before Select Committees of the House of Commons in the following Cases of Controverted Elections [inter alia] Horsham [and] Steyning* (1791). Refers to one case in Horsham, 1790, and two cases in Steyning, 1791.

C. Thomas-Stanford, *Sussex in the Great Civil War and the Interregnum 1642–1660* (1910).

William Albery, *A Parliamentary History of the Ancient Borough of Horsham, 1295–1885* (1927).

A. A. Dibben, *The Cowdray Archives Part I* (1960). Part of the introduction to this catalogue (pp. xx–xxvi) relates to Midhurst as a parliamentary borough.

L. P. Curtis, *Chichester Towers* (1966). Church and politics in eighteenth-century Sussex.

Roger B. Manning, *Religion and Society in Elizabethan Sussex* (1969).

Anthony Fletcher, *A County Community in Peace and War: Sussex, 1600–1660* (1975).

POVERTY

Farrant, pp. 38–40.

David Davies, *The Case of Labourers in Husbandry* (1795). With an appendix of accounts showing the earnings and expenses of labouring families, including data for Sidlesham (incorrectly shown as in Surrey), Funtington (incorrectly given as Tuntington) and North Mundham (incorrectly given as North Munden).

Rev. Arthur Young, *General View of the Agriculture of the County of Sussex* (2nd edn. 1808). The 1813 impression has been published in facsimile (1970), by David & Charles. Sections deal with wages, the cost of living and the poor, including details of the Gilbert Union Workhouse at Easebourne.

Anon., *Emigration: Letters from Sussex Emigrants, who sailed from Portsmouth, in April 1832 . . . for Upper Canada* (1833).

James Marr Brydone, *Narrative of a Voyage with a Party of Emigrants, sent out from Sussex, in 1834, by the Petworth Emigration Committee, to . . . Upper Canada* (1834).

A Carrier's Boy [Eli Hamshire], *The Source of England's Greatness, and the Source of England's Poverty* (4th edn. 1892). References to poverty in Sussex.

Mrs. Cobden Unwin, *The Hungry Forties: Life under the Bread Tax: descriptive letters and other testimonies from contemporary witnesses* (1904). Accounts of poverty and starvation, including a number relating to Heyshott.

The Twenty-Second Warden, *Sackville College* (1913). Founded in the early seventeenth century in East Grinstead as a charitable home for the poor.

Helena Hall, *William Allen, 1770–1843* (1953). Founder of a nineteenth-century allotment colony for the poor at Lindfield.

Jane M. Coleman, *Sussex Poor Law Records: A Catalogue* (1960). Includes an outline history of poor law legislation and brief details of how this affected poor relief and workhouses in the county.

Wendy Cameron, 'The Petworth Emigration Committee: Lord Egremont's Assisted Emigrations from Sussex to Upper Canada, 1832–1837' in *Ontario History*, vol. 65, no. 4 (December 1973), pp. 231–246.

PREHISTORIC, ROMAN AND MEDIEVAL

Arthur John Hubbard and George Hubbard, *Neolithic Dew-Ponds and Cattle-Ways* (3rd edn. 1916).

James Dunning, *The Roman Road to Portslade* (1925).

E. Cecil Curwen, *Prehistoric Sussex* (1929).

S. E. Winbolt and George Herbert, *The Roman Villa at Bignor, Sussex* (2nd edn. 1930).

J. H. Pull, *The Flint Miners of Blackpatch* (1932).

S. E. Winbolt, *With a Spade on Stane Street* (1936).

W. E. P. Done, *Looking Back in Sussex* (1953). The Manhood Peninsula and West Wittering from the prehistoric to the Domesday period.

E. Cecil Curwen, *The Archaeology of Sussex* (2nd edn. 1954).

Edward Done, *Chichester as the Romans called it* (Chichester Paper no. 7, 1957).

A. E. Wilson, *The Archaeology of Chichester City Walls* (Chichester Paper no. 6, 1957).

Gordon J. Copley, *An Archaeology of South-East England* (1958).

John Holmes, *Chichester: The Roman Town* (Chichester Paper no. 50, 1965).

I. D. Margary, *Roman Ways in the Weald* (3rd edn. 1965).

E. A. Fisher, *The Saxon Churches of Sussex* (1970).

Ronald Jessup, *South-East England* (1970).

Barry Cunliffe, *Excavations at Fishbourne: Volume I: The Site. Volume II: The Finds* (1971).

Barry Cunliffe, *Fishbourne: A Roman Palace and its Gardens* (1971).

Alec Down and Margaret Rule, *Chichester Excavations I* (1971).

Ivan D. Margary, *Roman Sussex illustrated* (1971). Brief introductory essay.

Barry Cunliffe, *The Regni* (1973).

Alec Down, *Chichester Excavations II* (1974).

Alec Down, *Rescue Archaeology in Chichester* (1974).

Peter Drewett, *Rescue Archaeology in Sussex* (1974).

RELIGION

Farrant, pp. 40–41; Brent, Fletcher, McCann, pp. 40–50.

M. E. C. Walcott, *Memorials of Chichester* (1865).

W. R. W. Stephens, *Memorials of the South Saxon See and Cathedral Church of Chichester* (1876).

C. A. Swainson, *The History and Constitution of a Cathedral of the Old Foundation* (1880).

W. R. W. Stephens, *The South Saxon Diocese, Selsey–Chichester* (1881).

Thomas and Anne W. Marsh, *Some Records of the Early Friends in Surrey and Sussex* (1886).

George Hennessy, *Chichester Diocese Clergy Lists; or Clergy Succession from the earliest time to the year 1900* (1900). Clergy lists for each parish, including dignitaries of Chichester Cathedral and Chancellors of the diocese.

F. G. Bennett, R. H. Codrington and C. Deedes, *Statutes and Constitutions of the Cathedral Church of Chichester* (1904).

Arthur Ponsonby, *The Priory and Manor of Lynchmere and Shulbrede* (1920).

K. H. Macdermott, *Sussex Church Music in the Past* (2nd edn. 1923).

L. F. Salzman (ed.), *The Chartulary of the Priory of St. Peter at Sele* (1923). Benedictine foundation at Upper Beeding.

Irene Hernaman, *West Grinstead and Our Sussex Forefathers* (1924). Concentrates on the history of the Roman Catholic mission at West Grinstead.

J. S. Fletcher, *St. Wilfrid of Ripon* (1925).

E. B. Poland, *The Friars in Sussex, 1228–1928* (1928).

H. Willaert, *History of an Old Catholic Mission: Cowdray–Easebourne–Midhurst* (1928).

Caroline M. Duncan-Jones, *The Anglican Revival in Sussex* [c. 1933].

Caroline M. Duncan-Jones, *S. Richard of Chichester* (1953).

Ralph F. Chambers, *The Strict Baptist Chapels of England: Vol. II, The Chapels of Sussex* [1954].

N. Caplan, *Annals of Lindfield Congregational Church, 1810–1959* (1959).

J. S. Reynolds, *Providence Chapel, Chichester* (Chichester Paper no. 19, 1961).

A. G. Lough, *The Influence of John Mason Neale* (1962). Nineteenth-century ecclesiastic and founder of the Society of St. Margaret, East Grinstead.

Frank Buffard, *Kent and Sussex Baptist Associations* (1963).

Francis W. Steer, *The Church of St. John the Evangelist, Chichester, 1813–1963* (Chichester Paper no. 35, 1963).

Ronald Berman, *Henry King and The Seventeenth Century* (1964). Poet and divine, and Bishop of Chichester, 1642–70.

Joyce M. Horn, *John Le Neve: Fasti Ecclesiae Anglicanae, 1300–1541; Part VII: Chichester Diocese* (1964). *1541–1857; Part II: Chichester Diocese* (1971). The standard authority for the identification of the higher and cathedral clergy of the Church of England and of the offices held by them.

L. P. Curtis, *Chichester Towers* (1966). Church and politics in eighteenth-century Sussex.

David Newsome, *The Parting of Friends* (1966). Religious and personal crisis of the Oxford Movement in the lives of the Wilberforces and Henry Manning, united by marriage through the Sargent family of Lavington. Part of the unfolding controversy was set in and around Lavington.

Edward T. Stoneham, *Sussex Martyrs of the Reformation* (3rd edn. 1967).

R. B. Manning, *Religion and Society in Elizabethan Sussex* (1968).

REMINISCENCES AND DIARISTS

See also the Countryside and Folklore.

John Kent, *Records and Reminiscences of Goodwood and the Dukes of Richmond* (1896).

Henry Burstow, *Reminiscences of Horsham* (1911).

Nathaniel Paine Blaker, *Sussex in Bygone Days* (1919).

A. J. Rees, *Old Sussex and Her Diarists* (1929).

Philip C. Yorke, *The Diary of John Baker* (1931). Eighteenth-century barrister of the Middle Temple and Solicitor General of the Leeward Islands. The son of a Chichester grocer, there are many Sussex references, especially to Horsham.

E. Robinson and J. S. Heward, *Reminiscences of Littlehampton* (1933).

A. Longley, *Alexandra Terrace* (1960). Life in Worthing in the nineteenth and twentieth centuries.

C. A. Grigg, *Memories of Steyning* (1967).

M. J. Leppard (ed.), *Reminiscences of East Grinstead, 1893–1914* (1973).

A Hundred Years of Harting Life, 1850–1950: A Symposium (1973). Harting Paper no. 4.

F. C. Johnson (ed.), *Harting 1850–1950: A Further Selection* (1974). Harting Paper no. 5.

Kenneth Neale, *Victorian Horsham: The Diary of Henry Michell, 1809–1874* (1975).

Irene Wilson (ed.), *Memories of Itchenor* (1975).

SMUGGLING

Farrant, p. 32.

A Gentleman of Chichester, *A Full and Genuine History of the Inhuman and Unparalleled Murders of Mr. William Galley . . . and Mr. Daniel Chater . . . by Fourteen Notorious Smugglers* (5th edn., n.d. eighteenth century).

H. N. Shore, *Smuggling Days and Smuggling Ways* (1892).

Horace Smith *et. al., The Worthing Parade Number Two* (1954). A miscellany of articles in the Worthing Art Development Scheme, half of which is devoted to Sussex smuggling.

William [Durrant] Cooper, *Smuggling in Sussex* (1966). Reprinted from *Sussex Archaeological Collections*, vol. 10 (1858), pp. 69–94.

F. F. Nicholls, *Honest Thieves: The Violent Heyday of English Smuggling* (1973).

SPORT

Earl of March, *Records of the Old Charlton Hunt* (1910).

Geoffrey Sparrow, *The Crawley and Horsham Hunt* (c. 1930).

Earl Bathurst, *The Charlton and Raby Hunts* (1938).

H. F. and A. P. Squire, *Henfield Cricket and its Sussex Cradle* (1949).

Sir Home Gordon, *Sussex County Cricket* (1950).

H. F. and A. P. Squire, *Pre-Victorian Sussex Cricket* (1951).

George Washer, *A Complete Record of Sussex County Cricket, 1728 to 1957* (1958).

John Marshall, *Sussex Cricket: A History* (1959).

John Marshall, *The Duke who was Cricket* (1961). Life of the 2nd Duke of Richmond (1701–50)—of Goodwood—a formative influence in the history of the game.

Michael Seth-Smith, *Lord Paramount of the Turf: Lord George Bentinck, 1802–1848* (1971). Many references to the development of the Goodwood racecourse and the training stables.

David Hunn, *Goodwood* (1975). Set against the family background of the Dukes of Richmond and the development of the Goodwood estate since the seventeenth century, there is much about the history of the racecourse, with a chapter on the motor racing circuit.

TRADE AND INDUSTRY, INCLUDING MILLS

Farrant, pp. 36–37; Brent, Fletcher, McCann, pp. 20–24.

Anon., *Sussex Industries, A Series of Articles on the Principal and Peculiar Industries Practised in Sussex* [1883]. Articles on pottery, trugs, Selsey mousetraps, higgling (poultry fattening), Tunbridge Ware, ship building, gypsum, bricks and terra cotta, hops, lime burning, chemical works, wood industries, fishing, nursery and market gardens, pebbles and flints.

James Lowe-Warren, *Sussex Tokens* (1888).

Henry Cheal, *The Ships and Mariners of Shoreham* (1909).

Mary Cecilia Delany, *The Historical Geography of the Wealden Iron Industry* (1921).

Rhys Jenkins, *The Rise and Fall of the Sussex Iron Industry* (1921). Excerpt from the *Transactions of the Newcomen Society*, vol. 1 (1920–21).

R. Thurston Hopkins, *Old English Mills and Inns* (1927). Mostly refers to Sussex.

R. Thurston Hopkins, *Windmills* (n.d.). Two of the three sections are about Sussex mills.

M. I. Batten, *English Windmills*, vol. 2 (1930). Includes a record of Sussex mills.

G. M. Fowell, *Windmills in Sussex* (1930).

Ernest Straker, *Wealden Iron* (1931). Published in facsimile (1969), by David & Charles.

S. E. Winbolt, *Wealden Glass: The Surrey–Sussex Glass Industry* (1933).

Peter Hemming, *Windmills in Sussex* (1936).

W. Henry Brown, *Brighton's Co-operative Advance, 1828–1938* (n.d.). Refers to the spread of the Co-operative movement throughout Sussex.

H. R. Schubert, *History of the British Iron and Steel Industry from c. 450 B.C. to A.D. 1775* (1957). Numerous well-documented references to the Wealden iron industry.

Francis W. Steer, *Some Chichester Tradesmen, 1652–1839* (Chichester Paper no. 17, 1960).

Francis W. Steer, *The Chichester Needle Industry* (Chichester Paper no. 31, 1963).

B. C. Worssam, *Iron Ore Workings in the Weald Clay of the Western Weald* (1964). Offprint from *Proceedings of the Geological Association*, vol. 75, part 4, 1964.

G. H. Kenyon, *The Glass Industry of the Weald* (1967).

G. Fielder, *Hand Brickmaking: Method of Brickmaking Employed by Mr. A. V. G. Pycroft at his Chidham Brickfield* [1974].

TRANSPORT AND COMMUNICATIONS

Farrant, pp. 31–36; Brent, Fletcher, McCann, pp. 24–25.

William B. Prichard, *A Treatise on Harbours . . . and Plans for the Improvement of the Harbours on the South-Eastern Coast of England*, vol. 1 (1844). Includes an account of the development of the port of Arundel (Littlehampton Harbour), with proposals for its improvement.

J. B. Dashwood, *The Thames to the Solent by Canal and Sea* (1868).

William C. A. Blew, *Brighton and its Coaches: A History of the London and Brighton Road* (1894).

Henry Cheal, *The Ships and Mariners of Shoreham* (1909).

Charles G. Harper, *The Brighton Road* (3rd edn. 1922).

Henfrey Smail, *The Worthing Road and its Coaches* (2nd edn. 1944).

Henfrey Smail, *Coaching Times and After* (1948). Worthing and area.

Jeoffry Spence, 'Railways at Midhurst' in *The Railway Magazine* (March 1955), pp. 155–160.

H. C. P. Smail, 'The L.B. & S.C.R. West Coast Line' in *Railway World*, vol. 17 (1956), pp. 187–191; 217–220; 248–252; vol. 18 (1957), pp. 190–191.

F. D. Heneghan, *The Chichester Canal* (Chichester Paper no. 11, 1958).

H. P. White, *A Regional History of the Railways of Great Britain: Volume II: Southern England* (1961).

C. F. Dendy Marshall and R. W. Kidner, *History of the Southern Railway*, 2 vols. (2nd edn. 1963).

R. H. Clark, *A Southern Region Chronology and Record, 1803–1965* (1964).

I. D. Margary, *Roman Ways in the Weald* (3rd edn. 1965).

G. A. Viner, *The Postal History of Chichester, 1635–1900* (Chichester Paper no. 47, 1965).

Anon., *The Southdown Story: A history of Southdown Motor Services Limited, 1915–1965* (1965).

G. T. Moody, *Southern Electric, 1909–1968* (4th edn. 1968).

Charles Hadfield, *The Canals of South and South-East England* (1969).

E. C. B. Thornton, *South Coast Pleasure Steamers* (1969).

Nigel Wikeley and John Middleton, *Railway Stations: Southern Region* (1971).

John Farrant, *Mid-Victorian Littlehampton: the Railway and the Cross-Channel Steamers* (1972). Littlehampton Paper no. 4.

Rodney Symes and David Cole, *Railway Architecture of the South-East* (1972).

Edwin Course, *The Railways of Southern England: the Main Lines* (1973).

Jeremy Greenwood, *The Posts of Sussex: The Chichester Branch, 1250–1840* (1973). This branch included all of West Sussex.

C. F. Klapper, *Sir Herbert Walker's Southern Railway* (1973).

P. A. L. Vine, *London's Lost Route to the Sea* (3rd edn. 1973).

Edwin Course, *The Railways of Southern England: Secondary and Branch Lines* (1974).

Edward Griffith, *The Hundred of Manhood and Selsey Tramways later known as the West Sussex Railway, 1897–1935* (3rd edn. 1974).

TRAVELOGUES AND VISITORS' DESCRIPTIONS

Farrant, pp. 18–20; Brent, Fletcher, McCann, pp. 12–13.

Christopher Morris (ed.), *The Journeys of Celia Fiennes, c.* 1685–*c.* 1702 (1947).

G. D. H. Cole (ed.), *Daniel Defoe, A Tour Through the Whole Island of Great Britain, 1724–26* (1928).

William Gilpin, *Observations on the Coasts of Hampshire, Sussex and Kent made in . . . 1774* (1804).

John Stuart Mill, 'A Tour of Sussex in July, 1827' in *The Worthing Parade Number One* (1951), pp. 155–191.

William Cobbett, *Rural Rides* (1830). The 1853 edn. reprinted, with an introduction by Asa Briggs, 1957.

J. B. Dashwood, *The Thames to the Solent by Canal and Sea* (1868).

Timothy J. McCann (ed.), *Restricted Grandeur: Impressions of Chichester, 1586–1948* (1974).

WEST SUSSEX TOWNS

Farrant, pp. 29–31.

Arundel

M. A. Tierney, *The History and Antiquities of the Castle and Town of Arundel*, 2 vols. (1834).

21

G. W. Eustace, *Arundel: Borough and Castle* (1922).

Bognor Regis

Lindsay Fleming, *History of Pagham in Sussex*, 3 vols. (1949–50). In covering an area wider than the title suggests, this work includes many references to Bognor and its development as a seaside resort.

Burgess Hill

'Historicus', *Historical Notes of Burgess Hill from 1828 to 1891* [1891].

Albert H. Gregory, *The Story of Burgess Hill* (1933).

Albert H. Gregory, *Mid-Sussex through the Ages* (1938). Although rather a haphazard collection of miscellaneous information, without reference to sources, there is some useful material relating both to the development of Burgess Hill and Haywards Heath.

Chichester

Alexander Hay, *The History of Chichester* (1804). See Hilda Johnstone and Francis W. Steer, *Alexander Hay, Historian of Chichester* (Chichester Paper no. 20, 1961), and Nigel Wratten, *Index to Hay's History of Chichester (1804)* (1974).

A. Ballard, *A History of Chichester* (1898).

J. Low Warren, *Chichester Past and Present* (1901).

Thomas Gordon Willis, *Records of Chichester* (1928).

Thomas Sharp, *Georgian City* (1949).

Francis W. Steer (ed.), *The Memoirs of James Spershott* (Chichester Paper no. 30, 1962). Mid-eighteenth century to 1809.

Articles and Notes about Chichester in Sussex Archaeological Collections (vols. 1–100) and Sussex Notes and Queries (vols. 1–15) (Chichester Paper no. 38, 1963).

G. S. Burrows, *Chichester: A Study in Conservation* (1968).

Timothy J. McCann (ed.), *Restricted Grandeur: Impressions of Chichester, 1586–1948* (1974).

[Walter Hussey, ed.], *Chichester 900* (1975). Commemorating the nine hundredth anniversary of the foundation of the Cathedral. Some of the essays relate to the city generally, including Roman Chichester, the siege of Chichester, 1642, and to several personalities.

Bernard Price, *Bygone Chichester* (1975). Early photographs of the city.

East Grinstead

Wallace Henry Hills, *The History of East Grinstead* (1906).

(Note that an important source for local history information is the *Bulletin* of the East Grinstead Society (January 1969 to date). Copies are available for reference at the East Grinstead Library and the West Sussex Record Office.)

Haywards Heath

No history has yet been attempted, but see Albert H. Gregory, *Mid-Sussex Through the Ages* (1938).

Horsham

Dorothea E. Hurst, *The History and Antiquities of Horsham* (2nd edn. 1889).

Henry Burstow, *Reminiscenes of Horsham* (1911).

William Albery, *A Millennium of Facts in the History of Horsham and Sussex, 947–1947* (1947).

Christopher Fletcher (ed.), *Causeway: Horsham's Historical Magazine* (*c.* 1971). Popular and well-illustrated history of the town published in twelve monthly parts, plus an index.

Kenneth Neale, *Victorian Horsham: The Diary of Henry Michell, 1809–1874* (1975).

Littlehampton

E. Robinson and J. S. Heward, *Reminiscences of Littlehampton* (1933).

H. J. F. Thompson, *Little Hampton Long Ago* (1974).

Petworth

Rev. F. H. Arnold, *Petworth: A Sketch of its History and Antiquities* (1864).

Lord Leconfield, *Petworth Manor in the Seventeenth Century* (1954).

Shoreham-by-Sea

Henry Cheal, *The Story of Shoreham* (1921).

Steyning

Anna M. Butler, *Steyning, Sussex* (*c.* 1913).

Ernest W. Cox and Frank Duke, *In and Around Steyning* (1954).

C. A. Grigg, *Memories of Steyning* (1967).

H. M. and U. E. Lacey, *The Timber-Framed Buildings of Steyning* (1974).

Worthing

Marian Frost, *The Early History of Worthing* (1929).

F. W. H. Migeod (ed.), *Worthing: A Survey of Times Past and Present* (1938).

Edward Snewin and Henfrey Smail, *Glimpses of Old Worthing* (1945).

Henfrey Smail, *The Worthing Map Story* (1949).

L. M. Bickerton (ed.), *Worthing: A brief account of the history of the town from Neolithic times to the present day* (3rd edn. 1963). Worthing Museum publication no. 3.

H. R. H. Harmer and D. R. Elleray (eds.), *A Picture of Worthing* (1975). Early photographs of the town.

West Sussex Villages

Village and parish histories will be located by reference to the bibliographies listed on page 1 of this handbook, and to catalogue entries in the various libraries in the county, and the East and West Sussex Record Offices at Lewes and Chichester.

DIRECTORIES

There are three principal holdings of county directories in West Sussex:

Chichester Library

 1852; 1858; 1862; 1867; 1874; 1878; 1890; 1895; 1899; 1903; 1905;
 1907; 1909; 1915; 1918; 1922; 1924; 1930; 1934; 1938.

West Sussex Record Office

 1839; 1855; 1858; 1862; 1866; 1874; 1882; 1887; 1895; 1899; 1905;
 1907; 1909; 1913; 1915; 1918; 1922; 1927; 1930; 1934; 1938.

Worthing Library

 1839; 1855; 1858; 1866; 1874; 1878; 1890; 1895; 1899; 1903; 1905;
 1907; 1909; 1911; 1913; 1915; 1922; 1927; 1930; 1934; 1938.

Apart from the 1839 directory by James Pigot, and the 1858 directory by
F. R. Melville, the above three lists refer to the uniform *Kelly's directories*.
(The editions up to 1878 were published as *Kelly's Post Office directories*.)
They list, by place, the names of principal landowners and inhabitants,
farms, commercial businesses etc. Each list is prefaced by a brief topo-
graphical/historical and general description, which, where relevant, con-
cludes with a list of public establishments, public officers, schools, posting
houses, carriers, etc. The Melville and Kelly's directories each include a
useful selection of advertisements and an appendix of classified trades.

There are further holdings of Sussex directories in Brighton Reference
Library, East Sussex County Library Headquarters, Lewes, East Sussex
Record Office, Lewes, Hove Reference Library and the Sussex Archaeological Society, Lewes. For a list of Sussex directories and their locations
throughout the county, and elsewhere, see John H. Farrant, *Sussex
Directories, 1784–1940*, 2nd edition (1975). As well as county directories,
this lists directories for individual towns. For West Sussex these towns
are Arundel, Bognor, Chichester, Crawley, East Grinstead, Haywards
Heath, Horsham, Littlehampton, Shoreham and Worthing.

At Brighton the holding includes a Pigot directory for Sussex dated earlier
than those at the West Sussex Record Office and Worthing Library. This
is the Sussex section of Pigot's *London and Provincial Directory for 1826–7*.

An earlier directory is *Bailey's British Directory; or, Merchants' and
Traders' Useful Companion, for the Year 1784*, published in four volumes.
No volumes exist in any Sussex reference libraries; they may be consulted
in London at the Guildhall Library, the British Library (an imperfect
copy), and the Institute of Historical Research, University of London
(vol. 4 only). The Sussex entries are for Arundel, Battle, Brighton,
Chichester, Eastbourne, Horsham, Itchenor, Lewes, Midhurst, Petworth,
Shoreham and Steyning. An edited entry relating to Chichester (from
vol. 4) is printed in Francis W. Steer's, *Some Chichester Tradesmen, 1652–
1839* (Chichester Paper no. 17, 1960).

At the West Sussex Record Office there are photocopies of entries relating
to Chichester from the following directories:

 Peter Barfoot and John Wilkes, *The Universal British Directory*, vol. 2
 (1793, revised edn. 1797–8).
 William Holden, *Annual London & County Directory*, vol. 2 (1811).

James Pigot, *London & Provincial New Commercial Directory, 1823–4*, (1824).

William Robson, *Commercial Directory of London & the Six Home Counties*, 19th edn. (1839).

The standard work on early directories is by Jane E. Norton, *Guide to the National and Provincial Directories of England and Wales, excluding London, published before 1856* (1950).

GUIDE BOOKS

Although their historical commentary is often inaccurate, they are useful for their contemporary information. Contents typically include information on population, institutions, place and price of lodgings, communications, etc., e.g. *The Visitors' Guide to Bognor and its vicinity* (1859). In West Sussex there are good collections of guides at Chichester and Worthing Libraries and the West Sussex Record Office.

NEWSPAPERS

The most extensive collection in the county is preserved at Brighton Reference Library. The national collection of local newspapers is at the British Newspaper Library, Colindale, London. Chichester Library has a card index of the Sussex holding at Colindale.

The select list below gives the library or record office location of the following newspapers, or microfilm copies. The inclusion of a year does not necessarily indicate that the series is complete for that year, although this is so in most cases. Microfilm copies are indicated by the dates in italics.

Bognor Regis Observer	*1890–1974*	Chichester
(formerly *Bognor Observer*)	1965 to date	Bognor
	1886–90; 1900–1901;	West Sussex
	1905–27; 1929 to date	Record Office
Bognor Regis Post	*1924–1974*	Chichester
	1965 to date	Bognor
Brighton Daily News	1869–79	Brighton
Brighton & Sussex Daily Post & Hove Chronicle	1876–86	Brighton
Brighton Examiner	1853–5; 1857–95	Brighton
Brighton Fashionable & Local Register	1823	Brighton
Brighton Gazette (incorporated with the *Southern Weekly News*, 1926–33)	1821 to date	Brighton
Brighton Guardian	1827–8; 1834–1901	Brighton
Brighton & Hove Herald (formerly *Brighton Herald*)	1806–7; 1826–31; 1836–85; 1888–1971 *1918–71*	Brighton Hove
The Brightonian	1880–4	Brighton
Brighton Patriot	1835; *1835–9*	Brighton

Chichester Express	*1863–1902*	Chichester
Chichester Journal	*1860–64*	Chichester
Chichester Observer	1888 (commences no. 30); 1889; 1891–92; 1895–96; 1900–1901; 1904–09; 1911–27; 1929 to date	West Sussex Record Office
Crawley Observer	*1954–1972*	Chichester and Crawley
Evening Argus	1956 to date	Brighton
Hampshire Telegraph & Sussex Chronicle (formerly *Portsmouth Telegraph*, now *Hampshire Telegraph* series)	1811–16 1799–1848; 1875 to date; *1849–74* 1817–18	Brighton Portsmouth West Sussex Record Office
Lancing and Shoreham Times (changed to *Shoreham, Lancing and District Times*, 24.1.36)	1935–37	West Sussex Record Office
Lewes & Brightelmston Paquet & Weekly Advertiser	1789–90	Brighton
Littlehampton & Arundel News	1875–91 1906–7; 1910–14	Littlehampton Brighton
Littlehampton Observer	1909–27; 1929–38	West Sussex Record Office
Midhurst Times	1904; 1920–22; 1925–35	West Sussex Record Office
Midhurst and Petworth Times (changed to *Midhurst and Petworth Observer*, 3.1.64)	1935–49; 1951 to date	West Sussex Record Office
Southern Weekly News (see *Brighton Gazette* above)	1912–15	Brighton
Sussex Advertiser	1822–97; 1901–5	Brighton
Sussex Agricultural Express	1837 1837–1902 1837–46	Brighton East Sussex Record Office Hastings
Sussex Chronicle & Chichester Advertiser	1803	Chichester
Sussex County Herald	1913–38	East Sussex Record Office
Sussex Daily News (formerly *Brighton Daily News*, see above)	*1880–1956* *1881–1956* *1895–1900*; *1907–1956*	Brighton Hove Worthing
Sussex Express	1843–4; 1861; 1863–85; 1887–90; 1902; 1905–6; 1911; 1913–15 1903–38	Brighton East Sussex Record Office

Sussex Express & County Herald	1939–72	East Sussex Record Office
Sussex Weekly Advertiser or *Lewes Journal* (the first county newspaper[1])	1749(commences no. 157); 1751–2; 1758–64; 1769–84; 1786–1822	Brighton
	1749–1822	Chichester
	1749–1822	Hove
	1749–1822; 1769–1818	Worthing
West Sussex County Times (formerly *Horsham Advertiser*)	1871 to date	Horsham
West Sussex Gazette[2]	*1860–95; 1898–1910; 1912–14*	Bognor College of Education
	1860–95; 1897–1910; 1912–23	Brighton
	1860–1923; 1959–74	Chichester
	1860–87	West Sussex Record Office
	1860–87	Worthing
Worthing Gazette	1883–89; 1909 to date; *1889–1935*	Worthing
Worthing Herald	1920 to date	Worthing
Worthing Intelligencer	1890–93; 1898; 1902	Worthing
Worthing Monthly Record (*Worthing Record and Town & Country Newspaper* from 30 June 1855)	1853–6	Worthing

The following newspaper offices kindly permit access to their back numbers:

Crawley & District Observer 12 the Boulevard, Crawley (This paper was formerly known as the *Surrey & Sussex Courier*)	1945 to date
Mid-Sussex Times 19–23 Boltro Road, Haywards Heath	1881 to date
West Sussex Gazette 53 High Street, Arundel	1853 to date

Note that in all cases an appointment must be made before a visit. In the case of the *West Sussex Gazette* a small fee is usually charged.

DECENNIAL CENSUS RETURNS

Since 1801 there has been a census of the population every ten years, except in 1941. The returns are invaluable for showing the exact population of towns and villages at a given time, with much supplementary

[1] See Arthur Beckett, 'The First Sussex Newspaper' in *Sussex County Magazine*, vol. 15 (1941), pp. 247–254.

[2] See F. V. Wright, *A Hundred Years of the West Sussex Gazette, 1853–1953* (1953).

personal information such as occupations. The original Enumeration Schedules for 1841, 1851, 1861 and 1871 are available at the Public Record Office, Chancery Lane, London, WC2A 1LR (students' tickets obtainable on written application to the secretary). These Schedules are particularly valuable from 1851, since when it has been a requirement to provide exact information on age, birthplace, house numbers, and the relationship to the head of the family. Enumeration abstracts based on the Schedules were published as Parliamentary Papers. The Sussex abstracts for 1801 and 1821 are available at the West Sussex Record Office. The series for the period 1801–1931, and population statistics from the National Registration Act 1939, are available at the East Sussex Record Office.

The 1851 Enumeration Schedule is on microfilm at the West Sussex Record Office, covering all West Sussex parishes. The 1861 Enumeration Schedule is on microfilm at the East Sussex Record Office, and includes the following West Sussex parishes:

Botolphs, Coombes, Cowfold, Crawley, Kingston-by-Sea, New Shoreham, Old Shoreham, Sompting and Southwick, plus those parishes transferred to the county by local government re-organisation in 1974 (see page v).

Both the 1851 and 1861 Schedules covering the entire county of Sussex are on microfilm at Brighton Reference Library. Microfilm copies for the 1841 and 1871 Schedules are on order for this library from the Public Record Office (1975).

Population totals for individual Sussex parishes, 1801–1901, are listed in *Victoria County History, Sussex*, volume 2, pp. 217–28. See also Maurice Beresford, *The Unprinted Census Returns of 1841, 1851, 1861* (1966), and Inter-departmental Committee on Social and Economic Research, *Guides to Official Sources No. 2, Census Reports of Great Britain, 1801–1931* (1951).

OTHER PARLIAMENTARY PAPERS

Before and well into the nineteenth century, Parliament conducted its investigations through Select Committees, later by Royal Commissions and Departmental Committees. The published reports held at the West Sussex Record Office provide details of various social, economic and political problems of the nineteenth and twentieth centuries, often with useful Sussex references. In the following list the suffixes *R* and *M* indicate *Report* and *Minutes* respectively.

Boundaries and Wards of Certain Boroughs and Corporate Towns, 1837, *R*.

Boundary Commission, 1917, *R*. (Volume 2 only.)

Game Laws, 1872, *M*; 1873, *R, M*.

Gaols and Houses of Correction, 1863, *R, M*.

Ecclesiastical Courts Commission, 1883, *R, M*.

Ecclesiastical Revenues, 1835, *R*.

Habitual Drunkards, 1872, *R, M*.

Inclosure Act, 1869, *R, M*.

Licencing Statistics, 1912–13, *R*; 1915–20, *R*; 1922–8, *R*.

Local Government, 1923–9, *M*; 1925, *R*; 1929, *R*.

Plate I

Esau and Jacob.

Brother Electors,

You have doubtless read the story of Esau and Jacob in the Bible. Esau was a hairy Man, (not unlike many of you on a Saturday even;) Jacob was a smooth man. Esau came from the field and was faint, and asked his Brother for some pottage, but the wily Jacobite refused, unless he would that day sell to him his Birthright; and

" Esau did sell it, and despised his Birthright."

Be not, in this respect, my fellow Electors, like Esau; sell not this day to the Smooth Man, (the head of the firm of the three S.'s,) your birthright for a

GALLON OF BEER.

This same Smooth Man, I am informed, once addressed the Electors of Midhurst, thus; " I never approach this venerable and re- " spectable Borough, without feelings of re- " spect and affection"—(placing his hand on his heart)—Was he laughing at them, or was he serious—Be not you deluded by

Cant and Humbug.

Enough for the present, you may probably, before the day of Election, hear again from

Your Well-wisher,

AN ELECTOR.

Chichester, July 5, 1830.

Williams and Pullinger, Printers.

Broadsheet published during the Chichester election of 1830 (M.P. 136).

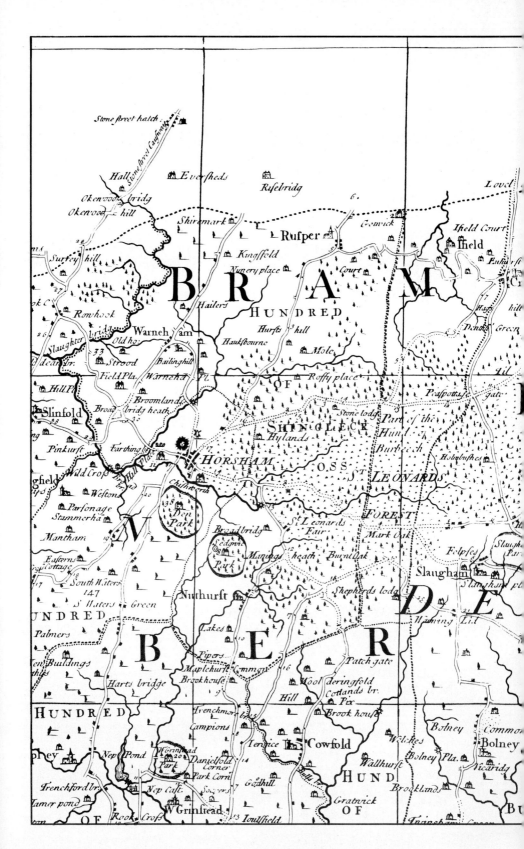

Section of *An Actual Survey of the County of Sussex* by Richard Budgen, 1724

Plate II

Plate III

JUVENILE RESEARCHES,

OR A

DESCRIPTION OF SOME OF THE PRINCIPAL Towns in the Western part of Sussex, and the borders of Hants.

INTERSPERSED WITH VARIOUS PIECES OF POETRY, BY A SISTER: and illustrated by numerous wood engravings executed by the Author.

The whole being composed and printed, BY A BOY OF 14.

"I pencill'd things I saw,
And profited by things I heard."

EASEBOURNE.

1835.

Frontispiece and title page of *Juvenile Researches* . . . . written and printed by Howard Dudley, aged fourteen, of Easebourne, 1835.

Police Powers and Procedure, 1928–9, *M.*

Poor Law, Abstract of the Answers and Returns to the Act for procuring returns relative to the expense and maintenance of the poor in England, 1805, *R.*

Poor Law, 1834–47, *R*; 1860, *R*; 1909, *R.*

Small Holdings, 1913, *R*; 1919, *R.*

State and Condition of the Cathedral and Collegiate Churches in England and Wales, 1854, *R. Appendix*, 1854, *R.*

Of the following three reports, which relate solely to Sussex, the first two are held by Chichester Library, the third by the West Sussex Record Office.

Sussex Charities, *c.* 1837.

Sussex Prisons, 1830.

Sussex Turnpike Trusts, 1852 (photocopy only).

Of the following two reports, Sussex extracts, in the form of photocopies, are available at the West Sussex Record Office.

Poor Law Commission, 1834. (The outcome of this report, published as a series of Appendices to the 1834 Poor Law Report, was the legislation embodied in the Poor Law Amendment Act, 1834.)

Gaols and Houses of Correction, 1835.

For students working on Parliamentary Papers there are two useful handbooks:

P. Ford and G. Ford, *A Guide to Parliamentary Papers* (1955).

W. R. Powell, *Local History from Blue Books: A Select List. Sessional Papers of the House of Commons* (Historical Association Pamphlet no. 64, 1962).

ACTS OF PARLIAMENT

Public general acts are available from Magna Carta to 1939 (as printed in bound volumes since 1762), and local and private acts from 1889 (i.e. since the formation of the administrative county of West Sussex) to 1923 and 1933 respectively. Public general acts, 1889 to date, may be consulted at Chichester Library.

At the West Sussex Record Office there is a miscellaneous collection of pre-1889 local and private acts relating to, *inter alia*, inclosure, turnpikes, railways, rivers, canals, gas, ports and private estates in West Sussex. See card index. Bound volumes of all printed local and private acts since 1798 are at the East Sussex Record Office.

POLL BOOKS

For elections before the 1872 Ballot Act these list those qualified to vote and the candidates for whom they voted. Poll books marked * refer to manuscript volumes, and those marked † refer to those that include supplementary information on the course of the election, with speeches, notices, squibs, etc. This list indicates those books held at Chichester Library (CHI), the West Sussex Record Office (WSRO), and Worthing Library (W).

The earliest recorded poll book for the county, for 1705, in manuscript, is held in the library of the Sussex Archaeological Society, Lewes. This has been transcribed and printed in volume 4 of the Sussex Record Society series (1905).

County

1734 (WSRO; W); 1774 (CHI; WSRO); 1820† (CHI; WSRO; W).

Arundel

1741* (WSRO).

Chichester

1781* (WSRO); 1782 (WSRO); 1784 (WSRO); 1791* (WSRO); 1793* (WSRO); 1823 (WSRO); 1826† (WSRO); 1830† (CHI; WSRO; W); 1831* (WSRO).

Midhurst

1708* (WSRO); 1710* (WSRO); 1711* (WSRO); 1716* (WSRO); 1735/6* (WSRO); 1737/8* (WSRO); 1741* (WSRO); 1744* (WSRO); 1747* (WSRO); 1754* (WSRO).

New Shoreham and the Rape of Bramber

1837* (WSRO); 1841† (W); 1865 (WSRO).

Western Division of Sussex

1837 (WSRO).

ELECTORAL REGISTERS

From the 1832 Reform Act an annual register was kept of persons entitled to vote. These list, by polling districts, the name, place of residence (larger houses are named, and later registers give street/road and number) and the nature and situation of the voting qualification. The West Sussex Record Office series is for 1832, 1835, 1838/9, 1842/3 to date.

SPECIALIST LIBRARIES IN THE WEST SUSSEX RECORD OFFICE

All the books in these collections are indexed in the comprehensive Record Office indexes of printed material, by authors, persons, places and subjects.

The Crookshank Collection

A collection of Sussex books, collected and presented to the Record Office by the Rev. A. C. Crookshank. Notable for the works of Blake and Hayley and their circle, and for books printed in Chichester. See Francis W. Steer, *The Crookshank Collection* (1960).

The Fuller Library

A collection of Sussex books collected by and presented in memory of Captain A. W. Fuller. Notable for Chichester books. Typescript list in the Search Room.

The Eric Gill Collection

A collection of books written or illustrated by Eric Gill, together with engravings, drawings and sculptures, presented by his family and friends. See Noel H. Osborne, *The Eric Gill Memorial Collection* (Chichester Paper no. 51, 1967).

The Hilda Johnstone Library

The library of the distinguished historian and former honorary archivist to the Bishop of Chichester, has been deposited in the Record Office. Notable for the collection of her works and for offprints of the works of her friends, colleagues and students. Typescript list in the Search Room.

The Mitford Library

Part of the Library of the Mitford family, once at Pitshill in Tillington. Typescript list in the Search Room.

UNPUBLISHED THESES

The majority of the following historical and geographical theses relating to Sussex are available for consultation at the appropriate university, or, in some cases, for reference *via* the Inter Library Loan Service. Students requiring these through this service should, in the first instance, contact their local library.

Copies of those theses marked with an asterisk * are available for reference in the Library of the Sussex Archaeological Society, Lewes.

A. M. Melville, The Pastoral and Local Wool Trade of Medieval Sussex, 1085–1485. (London M.A.) 1931.

F. G. Morris, Physical Controls in the historical geography of the Sussex Ports. (London M.A.) 1931.

Alice F. A. Mutton, An analysis of some of the interactions of geography and history in the Arun and Adur Valleys. (London M.A.) 1931.

H. C. K. Henderson, The Agricultural Geography of the Adur basin in its regional setting. (London Ph.D.) 1935.

A. J. Bull, Studies in the Geomorphology of the South Downs. (London Ph.D.) 1937.

E. Cook, The agricultural geography of West Sussex. (Liverpool M.A.) 1939.

E. W. H. Briault, The historical geography of a part of East Sussex. (London Ph.D.) 1939.

H. B. Smith, An historical study of the agriculture of part of south-eastern Sussex from 1780. (London M.A.) 1940.

R. B. K. Perch, The organisation of a college of secular priests as illustrated by the records of the college of the Holy Trinity, Arundel, 1380–1544. (London M.A.) 1942.

J. M. B. Fradin, Ralph Neville, Bishop of Chichester and Chancellor. (Oxford B.Litt.) 1942.

Margaret Coleman, Celtic settlement and agriculture in Central Sussex. (London M.A.) 1944.*

H. F. Pearmain, Horsham and its functions, local and regional, past, present and future. (London M.A.) 1944.

Madelaine J. Steventon, A study of landowners and their estates in Essex, Kent, Surrey and Sussex, based on the assessments for the Land Tax of 1412. (Oxford B.Litt.) 1949.

B. W. Sparks, A Contribution to the Geomorphology of the South Downs. (London M.A.) 1949.

D. K. Worcester, East Sussex landownership: the structure of rural society in an area of old inclosure, 1733–1787. (Cambridge Ph.D.) 1950.*

E. J. McDermott, The Life of Thomas Stapleton, 1535–1598. (London M.A.) 1950.

H. C. Brookfield, A Regional Study of urban development in coastal Sussex since the eighteenth century. (London Ph.D.) 1950.

Gwendolen J. Fuller, A geographical study of the development of roads through the Surrey-Sussex Weald to the south coast, during the period 1700–1900. (London Ph.D.) 1950.

F. C. Walden-Aspy, Edward Story, Bishop of Chichester, 1422–1503; a study in fifteenth century ecclesiastical administration. (London M.A.) 1951.

J. M. W. Bean, The estates of the Percy family, 1416–1537. (Oxford D.Phil.) 1952.

J. C. K. Cornwall, The agrarian history of Sussex, 1560–1640. (London M.A.) 1953.*

G. R. Batho, The household accounts of Henry Percy, ninth earl of Northumberland (London M.A.) 1953.

Margaret M. Cramp, The parliamentary representation of the Sussex boroughs, Bramber, Midhurst, Lewes, Rye and Winchelsea, 1754–1768. (Manchester M.A.) 1953.

E. M. Yates, A contribution to the historical geography of the western Weald. (London M.Sc.) 1953.

Jane G. Pilmer, The history and archaeology of Roman Chichester. (Durham M.Litt.) 1954.

D. G. Lerpinière, Some aspects of the life and work of a Reformation Bishop as revealed in the writings of Richard Sampson, Bishop of Chichester. (London M.A.) 1954.

J. H. Andrews, Geographical aspects of the maritime trade of Kent and Sussex, 1650–1750. (London M.A.) 1954.

Joyce E. Mousley, Sussex country gentry in the reign of Elizabeth. (London Ph.D.) 1955.

R. F. Hunnisett, The medieval coroner, 1194–1487, with special reference to the County of Sussex. (Oxford D.Phil.) 1956.

Alison Gilbert, The political correspondence of Charles Lennox, third Duke of Richmond. (Oxford D.Phil.) 1956.

Marie Clough, The estates of the Pelham family in East Sussex before 1500. (Cambridge Ph.D.) 1956.*

A. Rogers, The parliamentary representation of Surrey and Sussex, 1377–1422. (Nottingham M.A.) 1957.

E. A. Course, The evolution of the railway network of South East England. (London Ph.D.) 1958.

J. A. Barrett, The Seaside Resort Towns of England and Wales. (London Ph.D.) 1958.

J. L. M. Gulley, The Wealden Landscape in the Early Seventeenth Century and its antecedents. (London Ph.D.) 1960.

H. Mayr-Harting, The Bishops of Chichester and the administration of their diocese from the Norman Conquest to 1207, with a collection of acta. (Oxford D.Phil.) 1961.

D. W. Gramolt, The coastal marshland of East Sussex between the seventeenth and mid-nineteenth centuries. (London M.A.) 1961.

G. L. Barnard, The Oliver Whitby School, Chichester; a study of the repercussions of contemporary trends, social and educational, in the fortunes of the school, 1702–1904. (London Ph.D.) 1961.

Florence A. Hamblin, Horsham; a geographical study. (London M.A.) 1962.

P. F. Brandon, The common lands and wastes of Sussex. (London Ph.D.) 1963.*

D. Burtenshaw, The Sussex gap towns, a geographical analysis. (London M.A.) 1963.

R. J. W. Swales, Local Politics and parliamentary representation of Sussex, 1529–1558. (Bristol Ph.D.) 1964.

J. S. Macauley, Richard Montague, Caroline Bishop, 1575–1641. (Cambridge Ph.D.) 1964.

Judith Wooldridge, Alciston Manor, Sussex, in the later middle ages. (Bristol M.A.) 1965.

G. O. Cowley, Sussex Market Towns, 1550–1750. (London M.A.) 1965.

D. G. Dallimore, Transport and Town Planning with special reference to Brighton. (London M.Sc.) 1965.

J. N. Hutchinson, The stability of cliffs composed of soft rocks with particular reference to the coasts of South East England. (Cambridge Ph.D.) 1966.

D. M. King, Changes in associational life consequent upon population increase [the village of Newick] (Sussex M.A.) 1966.

B. Thompson, The growth of manufacturing in the Brighton conurbation, 1901–1963 (Sussex M.Phil.) 1966.

I. G. Wilkinson, The influence of demographic change on social provision in selected East Sussex villages. (Sussex M.A.) 1966.

M. Wright, The Cinque Port Towns: A comparative geographical study. (London Ph.D.) 1965.

Monju Dutt, The agricultural labourers revolt of 1830 in Kent, Surrey and Sussex. (London Ph.D.) 1967.

T. M. Kemnitz, Chartism in Brighton. (Sussex D.Phil.) 1969.

D. Haslam, The location of manufacturing industry in five counties of South East England, with special reference to the period, 1960–1968. (LSE Ph.D.) 1970.

A. G. Woodcock, The Mesolithic of South East England. (Leicester M.A.) 1970.

K. J. Barton, The development and dating of the medieval pottery of Sussex. (Southampton M.Phil.) 1971.*

I. P. Jolliffe, Coastline changes, beach nourishment and sea defences, with special reference to the coastline of Sussex and Kent. (London Ph.D.) 1971.

R. M. Luis, Hydrogeology of part of East Sussex. (London Ph.D.) 1971.

B. M. Short, Agriculture in the High Weald of Kent and Sussex, 1850 to 1953. A case study in the application of multivoriate techniques in the field of Historical Geography. (London Ph.D.) 1973.

C. E. Brent, Employment, Land Tenure and Population in Eastern Sussex, 1540–1640 (Sussex D.Phil.) 1974.

P. R. Harrington, The private press in Sussex. (Library Association F.L.A.) 1974.

S. J. Lander, The Diocese of Chichester, 1508–1558; episcopal reform under Robert Sherburne and its aftermath. (Cambridge Ph.D.) 1974.

PART II PICTORIAL AND ORAL SOURCES

MAPS AND PLANS

There is an extensive and finely executed collection of county, parish, town and estate maps available at the West Sussex Record Office, dating from the late sixteenth century. For a list of the majority of maps at the East Sussex, and West Sussex Record Offices, and the Sussex Archaeological Society, Lewes, see Francis W. Steer, *A Catalogue of Sussex Estate and Tithe Award Maps* (1962), and *A Catalogue of Sussex Maps* (1968). Besides those at the Record Offices, there are important map collections at Brighton, Hove and Worthing Libraries.

ORDNANCE SURVEY MAPS

The Ordnance Survey was founded for military purposes in 1791 by the 3rd Duke of Richmond—of Goodwood—with the original object of preparing a map of the United Kingdom on a scale of 1″ to one mile. A controversy followed about the most suitable scale for the initial basic surveys from which the 1″ maps were produced, with the result that a 6″ survey was begun in Ireland in 1824, and a 25″ survey in County Durham in 1853. The more modern $2\frac{1}{2}$″ series also derives from military purposes, from maps prepared for use during the 1939–45 War. Town plans on various scales have also been published by the Ordnance Survey since the 1840s, and also geological, soil survey, land utilisation and other thematic maps.

Sir Charles Close, *The Early Years of the Ordnance Survey* (1926). Reprinted, with notes by J. B. Harley, by David & Charles (1969).

J. B. Harley and C. W. Phillips, *The Historian's Guide to Ordnance Survey Maps* (1964).

1″ Series

The two sheets for Sussex (which exclude some of the border parishes) were first published in 1813. *Sheet 9, Brighton*, covers the majority of West Sussex, and *Sheet 5, Hastings*, the extreme north-eastern parishes such as West Hoathly and Horsted Keynes. There are original sheets of both maps at the West Sussex Record Office (PM 31 and PM 313 respectively).

The surveyors' preliminary survey drawings, mostly at a scale of 2″ to one mile, are in the Map Room of the British Library, and often reveal features that do not appear on the published maps. For most of West Sussex these surveys were made during and after 1805, except for part of Mid-Sussex, including Horsham and Haywards Heath, which was surveyed in 1792 at a scale of 3″ to one mile. Photocopies of these West Sussex sheets are in the West Sussex Record Office (PM 280–285).

Subsequent surveys have resulted in the publication of a total of seven editions to the present. There are editions and revisions from 1813 available at the West Sussex Record Office.

The first edition of sheets 9 and 5 has been reproduced in facsimile (in 1969) by David & Charles, with additions to 1888 and 1884 respectively, including historical commentaries by J. B. Harley. A similar venture, but reproducing the original sheets without any later additions, has been inaugurated in 1975, with notes by J. B. Harley and Yolande O'Donoghue.

Volume 1 includes sheet 5, and volume 3, sheet 9. These volumes are published by Harry Margary, Lympne Castle, Kent.

Note that in 1974 the Ordnance Survey began the publication of a new map series—at a scale of approximately 1¼″ to one mile—which replaces the 1″ series.

2½″ Series

These are available for West Sussex, and date from 1946.

6″ Series

Sussex was first surveyed for this series between 1869 and 1875. First, second and subsequent editions are available.

The archaeological division of the Ordnance Survey has issued copies of this series with archaeological sites added in manuscript. Each site is supported by a card index, with brief information and bibliographic references. A set of maps and cards for West Sussex is held by Chichester Library.

25″ Series

As with the 6″ maps, Sussex was first surveyed for this series between 1869 and 1875. Most of the West Sussex sheets are held at the West Sussex Record Office. For availability see the indexes in the Map Room. There is a series of accompanying Books of Reference (1870–77) to indicate the area and use of each parcel of land, classified by parish. The up-to-date sheets of this series are available for public inspection at the West Sussex County Planning Office, County Hall, Chichester, by giving notice of an intended visit. These are the post-1945 *National Grid Series* which include the coastal strip, the extreme western border, the Petworth and Midhurst area, the Billingshurst and Horsham area, and the mid-Sussex area transferred to West Sussex in 1974. Also available at the County Planning Office is the *County Series* dating from 1912, covering certain rural parts of West Sussex for those areas not included in the *National Grid Series*. Many sheets of the earlier *County Series* are held in the West Sussex Record Office.

50″ Series

A post-1945 series covering the main urban areas of West Sussex is available for inspection at the County Planning Office, as above. This series covers the coastal conurbation from Pagham in the west to Southwick in the east; the West Sussex area of Haslemere, around Camelsdale; Chichester, Horsham, Crawley, and the central town area of East Grinstead. Sheets for Burgess Hill and Haywards Heath are in preparation.

10.56 feet to one mile — Town Plans

In the 1870s plans were published for Chichester, Horsham, Petworth and Worthing. Chichester (1875) and Petworth (1874) are in the West Sussex Record Office. (For Chichester the sheets are catalogued as PM 13, 120, 245–247; and for Petworth as PM 121.) A copy of the Horsham plan (1874) is at the offices of the Horsham District Council, Park House, North Street, Horsham (Engineer's and Surveyor's Department) and may be inspected by making prior application. A copy of the Worthing plan

(1875) is in the Borough Engineer's Department, Town Hall, Worthing. A reproduction of this is available for consultation in the map collection in the Worthing Reference Library.

Geological Series

Sheet 9 of the 1″ to one mile series showing geology was first published in 1864 by the Geological Survey of Great Britain. This edition is available at Chichester and Worthing Libraries. A revised edition was published in 1893 and is available at the West Sussex Record Office (PM 5). In the most recent editions issued at the same scale the entire county of West Sussex is covered in ten sheets, i.e.:

300 *Alresford*	301 *Haslemere*	302 *Horsham*	303 *Tunbridge*
316 *Fareham*	317 *Chichester*	318 *Brighton*	*Wells*
331 *Portsmouth*	332 *Bognor*	333 *Worthing*	

These ten sheets are available at Chichester Library.

Thematic Maps

A series is available at Chichester and Worthing Libraries, including types of farming, land classification, vegetation, local accessibility, gravel and sands, limestone including chalk, twentieth-century population changes.

County Maps

The following is a select list of county maps available at the West Sussex Record Office:

Christopher Saxton	1575	1″ to *c.* 5m.	Petworth House Archives 3531.
John Norden	1595	0.3″ to 1m.	PM 24.
John Speed	1611	1″ to *c.* 4m.	PM 118.
John Ogilby	1675	1″ to 1m.	The first detailed survey of the roads of England and Wales. For West Sussex these are strip maps of the London–Chichester, London–Arundel roads. PM 12.
Richard Budgen	1724 (1779 edn.)	¾″ to 1m.	The first county map to give topographical detail: roads, parks, churches, mills, important houses, sluices, quarries, iron furnaces, forges, etc. PM 47.
Thomas Yeakell and William Gardner	1778 –83	2″ to 1m.	Covers the southern part of Sussex in four sheets. Sheet 1: Hampshire-Littlehampton; Sheet 2: Tortington–Brighton. PM 48.
Thomas Yeakell, William Gardner and Thomas Gream	1795	1″ to 1m.	PM 46.

| Charles and John
Greenwood | 1825 | 1" to 1m. | PM 129. |
| William Figg | 1861 | 1" to 1m. | PM 14. |

Harry Margary (ed.), *Two Hundred and Fifty Years of Map-Making in the County of Sussex* (1970). This collection of reproductions of Sussex maps published between 1575 and 1825, with introductory notes by R. A. Skelton, includes the above-listed county maps, except the edition by Figg.

A sixteenth-century survey of the Sussex coastline showing the defences against invasion (the original of which is in the British Library, Department of Manuscripts, Add. MS. 57494), was published in facsimile in 1870 with notes by Mark Antony Lower: *A Survey of the Coast of Sussex made in 1587, With a view to its defence against Foreign Invasion, and especially against the Spanish Armada.*

Useful check-lists for printed maps relating to the county are:

Thomas Chubb, *The Printed Maps in the Atlases of Great Britain and Ireland: A Bibliography, 1570-1870* (1927; facsimile reprint by Dawsons of Pall Mall, 1966).

R. A. Skelton, *County Atlases of the British Isles, 1579-1703* (1970).

TOWN MAPS

This list indicates the dates of the earliest maps (either manuscript or printed) available in the county for the following West Sussex towns. As they were produced for a wide variety of administrative, legal or political purposes, rather than with the traveller in mind, detail is sometimes extremely selective and limited. They may be consulted at the West Sussex Record Office, unless otherwise stated.

Arundel	1778	At Arundel Castle; MS. RL5.
Bognor	*c.*1825	Add. MS. 4710.
Burgess Hill[1]	1845	TD/E77.
Chichester[2]	1595	PM 24 (facsimile copy).
Crawley	1839	TD/W155.
East Grinstead	1799	At East Sussex Record Office; De la Warr MS. 562.
Haywards Heath[3]	1845	TD/E91.
Horsham	1770	At Horsham Museum.
Littlehampton	1671/2	At Littlehampton Museum (nineteenth-century copy).
Midhurst	1632/3	Add. MS. 2096 (facsimile copy).
Petworth	1610	Petworth House Archives 3574.
New Shoreham	1811	QDP/W25.

[1] & [3] The early development of Burgess Hill and Haywards Heath, shortly after the opening of the railway in 1841, is shown on these Tithe Maps for the parishes of Keymer and Cuckfield respectively.

[2] For a reproduction of this earliest town plan of Chichester, by John Norden, see David J. Butler, *The Town Plans of Chichester, 1595-1898* (1972), p. 4.

| Steyning | 1639 | Wiston MS. 5591. |
| Worthing | 1814 | Published in John Evans, *Picture of Worthing*, vol. 1 (2nd edn. 1814).[1] |

INCLOSURE AWARD MAPS

The more intensive farming of the 17th, 18th and 19th centuries required a change from the customary techniques based on common fields and also the bringing into cultivation of open wasteland. They were changes either brought about by private agreement, or, increasingly from the 17th century, by Act of Parliament. An inclosure act resulted in an award to register the re-allotment of land. Each award, accompanied by a map, provides vital clues to the ownership, use and tenure of the land, as well as information on public and private carriage roads, bridle and footways, farms, house and field names, mills, pounds, quarries, pits, etc.

Unlike some counties, especially in the midlands, most of Sussex had been inclosed before the eighteenth century by private agreement, a transfer often recorded in earlier manorial documents. The total extent of common field inclosure by parliamentary act has been calculated as a mere 1.5% of the total area of the county; see W. E. Tate, *Sussex Inclosure Acts and Awards* (1950). Inclosure maps for West Sussex date between *c.*1769 and *c.*1872, and are available at the West Sussex Record Office for the following:

Aldingbourne; Amberley; Angmering; Ashington with Washington; Barnham; Bepton; Birdham; Bosham with Funtington; Boxgrove; Bury; Chidham; Chiltington, West; Chithurst; Clayton; Coldwaltham; Durrington; Eartham; Eastergate; Felpham; Findon; Grinstead, West, and Cowfold; Haywards Heath in Cuckfield; Horsham; Horsted Keynes; Houghton with South Stoke; Hunston; Ifield; Iping; Keymer with Balcombe with Worth; Lancing; Lavant, East and Mid; Littlehampton; Lyminster; Nuthurst; Oving; Poling; Pulborough; Pycombe; Rogate; Rudgwick; Rustington; Selsey; Sidlesham; Slindon; Southwick; Storrington; Stoughton; Tarring, West; Terwick; Thakeham with Sullington with Shipley with Itchingfield; Thorney, West; Walberton; Washington; Westbourne; Wisborough Green with Fittleworth; Wittering, West; Woolavington with Graffham.

The inclosure map and award for Broadwater is available for public inspection at the Borough Secretary's Department, Town Hall, Worthing, where there are also duplicate copies of the maps for Durrington and West Tarring. The inclosure records for Lindfield are in the East Sussex Record Office as part of the records of the manor of Framfield.

The authoritative study of the history of inclosure is by W. E. Tate, *The English Village Community and the Enclosure Movements* (1967).

TITHE AWARD MAPS

These maps resulted from the 1836 Tithe Commutation Act that converted tithe payments into money charges. Each parish was surveyed by a

---

[1] There are copies at Chichester and Worthing Reference Libraries and the West Sussex Record Office. See Henfrey Smail, *The Worthing Map Story* (1949), pp. 84–107. But also compare two earlier plans of the manor of Worthing, *c.*1805 and *c.*1810 (Add. MSS. 460, 461 respectively), the latter with details superimposed at a later date.

valuer to assess this charge, and the large scale maps produced for this purpose, mostly at a scale of 26.6″ to one mile, reveal a wealth of detail: farm and field names, the state of cultivation, common fields and meadows, boundary marks, names of roads, lanes, inns and public houses, wind and water mills, schools, marl pits, turnpike gates, kilns, workhouses, etc. For parishes in West Sussex the maps date between 1837 and 1859. The majority are between 1838 and 1840. For each map an award was made in the form of a schedule of tabulated information stating the owner and/or occupier of each parcel of land, its name and description, acreage and state of cultivation, and the amount of rent charge apportioned. Each parcel is related to the map by a key number.

Tithe maps for West Sussex are available at the West Sussex Record Office with the following exceptions: no maps were made for North Stoke and West Thorney, and those for South Ambersham, Lower Beeding and Houghton show only part of those parishes. For Chichester the parishes with awards were St. Bartholomew, St. Pancras and St. Peter the Great (Subdeanery); these three Chichester maps only include the areas of the city outside the walls. For West Tarring a reproduction only of the original map is available.

Tithe maps and awards for England and Wales may be consulted at the Public Record Office, Chancery Lane, London, WC2A 1LR. They are also available on microfilm at the Tithe Redemption Office, Inland Revenue Offices, Barrington Road, Worthing, BN12 4XP. This office is open to the public, by appointment, Monday to Friday, 9.00 a.m. to 4.00 p.m.

The tithe maps for both West and East Sussex parishes are reproduced on microfilm in the West Sussex Record Office.

For further information about these records see:

'The Records of the Tithe Redemption Commission' in *Journal of the Society of Archivists*, vol. 1 (1955–59), pp. 132–139.

H. C. Prince, 'The Tithe Surveys of the Mid-Nineteenth Century' in *The Agricultural History Review*, vol. 7 (1959), pp. 14–26.

E. A. Cox and B. R. Dittmer, 'The Tithe Files of the Mid-Nineteenth Century' in *The Agricultural History Review*, vol. 13 (1965), pp. 1–16.

DEPOSITED PLANS

By the end of the eighteenth century the Standing Orders of both Houses of Parliament required promoters of river improvements and canals to deposit with the Clerk of the Peace for the county or counties involved a copy of the plans, sections and books of reference of proposed works, giving owners and occupiers affected. This requirement was extended to include other engineering works that affected property rights. Since 1930 the required documents have been deposited with the Clerks, and since 1974, the Secretaries, of county councils. At the West Sussex Record Office there are deposited plans for the following groups:

River improvements and canals

Piers, harbours and coastal works

Turnpikes, roads and bridges

Railways

Waterworks

Gasworks

Gas and water combined schemes

Electricity

Tramways

Miscellaneous, such as Chichester Cattle Market and Worthing Post Office.

Certain of these public works represented by deposited plans, especially those for lines of communication, relate to both West and East Sussex, particularly since the alteration of the county boundary in April 1974. For example, many of the railway schemes for the London to Brighton route were aligned through what is now West Sussex to terminate in East Sussex. Such railway plans are in the East Sussex Record Office. If there is any doubt about a particular plan, searchers are advised to contact one of the two Sussex record offices before their visit to ensure its precise location. The West Sussex Record Office is planning (1975) to have microfilm copies of those plans in the East Sussex Record Office which relate to West Sussex.

ESTATE MAPS

In this category are probably some of the finest maps for the county. The most superb are undoubtedly the Goodwood Estate surveys by Thomas Yeakell and William Gardner made in the late eighteenth century for the 3rd Duke of Richmond.[1] These and other maps may be located through the West Sussex Record Office printed catalogues of the various estate archives and the two map catalogues. For a list of these catalogues see insert to this handbook.

DRAWINGS, PRINTS, PHOTOGRAPHS AND POSTCARDS

A small but growing collection of pictorial sources is available at the West Sussex Record Office. In addition there are extensive photographic and postcard collections at Brighton, Chichester, Hove and Worthing Libraries and at the Bognor Regis College of Education.

The Bognor Regis College of Education Library preserves the local history collection of the late Gerard Young (1912–1972), which, in addition to his fine collection of Sussex books and printed ephemera, includes extensive coverage of Bognor Regis and surrounding villages in engravings, photographs and postcards. Prior application to the Librarian for the use of this collection is essential.

The Brighton Reference Library collection includes the Sussex Photographic Survey, 1880–1940, arranged by place, with a crafts and industries section, and the important Madgwick collection of photographs relating to the London, Brighton and South Coast Railway Company.

---

[1] See T. R. Holland, 'The Yeakell and Gardner Maps of Sussex' in *Sussex Archaeological Collections*, vol. 95 (1957), pp. 94–104.

A large collection of photographs of West Sussex towns and villages, taken by Francis Frith & Co. of Reigate in the late nineteenth and early twentieth centuries, is held by Chichester Library. These are the original prints from which the company's postcards were produced. (For background details to the Frith postcard business and the disposal of these original prints see Bill Jay, *Victorian Cameraman: Francis Frith's Views of Rural England, 1850–1898* (1973).) The Library has also a series of aerial photographs on West Sussex towns and downland features.

Early photographs of East Grinstead, many with descriptive annotations, are held by East Grinstead Library.

At Hove Reference Library there are the papers of the late Frances Garnet, Viscountess Wolseley (1872–1936), which include 117 binders, each containing an extensive collection, of engravings, photographs and postcards supported by notes, newspaper cuttings, etc., arranged alphabetically by parish. The collection, which was started in 1924, is of particular value for the architectural history of smaller houses in the county. Many of the photographs were specially commissioned for Lady Wolseley's articles about Sussex houses in the *Sussex County Magazine*. Also at Hove there is a series of photographs of Sussex towns, villages and downland features photographed by the Cambridge Aerial Photographic Unit in the early 1950s.

A miscellaneous series of aerial photographs dating from 1945 is available for public inspection at the West Sussex County Planning Office,[1] County Hall, Chichester, including surveys of Arundel, Bognor, Chichester, Crawley, Horsham, Littlehampton, Pulborough and Wisborough Green, and two coastal surveys made in 1963 and 1965, covering from Hove to Havant, Hampshire, and from the coastline to the Downs. In 1971, in conjunction with the Census, the first complete survey of the entire county of West Sussex was undertaken, and prints are available for inspection at the County Planning Office. Copies may also be purchased. It should be noted that this survey of West Sussex anticipated local government re-organisation in 1974 and included the area transferred from East to West Sussex three years later.

Aerial photographs are also available from the Ordnance Survey, Air Photo Cover Group, Room N153, Romsey Road, Maybush, Southampton, SO9 4DH.

In 1975, in conjunction with European Architectural Heritage Year, the West Sussex Record Office embarked on a photographic survey of West Sussex towns and villages to create a permanent record for the future. The results should be available for reference at the Record Office by the spring of 1976.

Eighteenth and nineteenth century prints are in the following printed works:

James Rouse, *The Beauties and Antiquities of the County of Sussex* (1825).

Walter H. Godfrey and L. F. Salzman (eds.), *Sussex Views selected from the Burrell Collections* (1951).[2]

[1] Some duplicates, dated 1947–1949, are available in the Record Office.

[2] The Burrell Collection of topographical drawings of Sussex preserved at the British Museum is on microfilm at the West Sussex Record Office.

Frank Graham, *Sussex 100 Years Ago* (1969).

Good collections of nineteenth and early-twentieth century photographs have been published in the following:

Edward Snewin and Henfrey Smail, *Glimpses of Old Worthing* (1945).

M. J. Cutten and Francis W. Steer, *Changing Chichester* (Chichester Paper no. 24, 1961).

Charles White, *19th & early 20th Century Midhurst in old photographs* (1972).

James S. Gray, *Victorian and Edwardian Sussex from old photographs* (1973).

H. J. F. Thompson, *Little Hampton Long Ago* (1974).

H. R. H. Harmer and D. R. Elleray (eds.), *A Picture of Worthing* (1975).

Bernard Price, *Bygone Chichester* (1975).

Further useful sources for reproductions of engravings and photographs are the volumes of the *Sussex County Magazine* (1926–1956), and for photographs, the latest Sussex periodical, *Sussex Life* (since 1965 and proceeding). For the library locations of both publications see pages 6 and 7 of this handbook.

ORAL HISTORY

The West Sussex Record Office, in co-operation with the County Library Service, has started a tape archive scheme. The tapes will be catalogued and stored in the Record Office, and available for consultation here. Brighton Library has collected several tapes, and the Sussex Society for the Study of Labour History, with the sponsorship of the Brighton Trades Council, has launched a project to tape record the reminiscences of local people with long activity in the labour movement. Tapes of several recent series of talks on local history broadcast by Radio Brighton are held by Brighton Public Libraries and/or the University of Sussex Library. A memorandum on techniques and questions for use in interviewing is available from the West Sussex Record Office.

PART III DOCUMENTARY SOURCES

JUDICIAL AND ADMINISTRATIVE RECORDS

SESSIONS RECORDS

Until well into the nineteenth century the Justices of the Peace in Quarter
Sessions performed a wide range of administrative, as well as judicial,
functions—supervising parochial administration of roads and poor relief,
maintaining and inspecting prisons, houses of correction, and asylums,
supervising the constabulary, licensing alehouses, religious registration,
etc. See David J. Butler, *Quarter Sessions and the Justices of the Peace in
West Sussex* (1972). It should be noted that a number of Quarter Sessions
Records relating to West Sussex are in the East Sussex Record Office at
Pelham House, Lewes.

Quarter Sessions Rolls. These contain documents relating to business
transacted at each Quarter Session, and the Order Books (at the East
Sussex Record Office) provide a formal record of proceedings, the administrative orders, resolutions and judicial decisions. See B. C. Redwood,
Quarter Sessions Order Book, 1642–1649, Sussex Record Society, vol. 54,
(1954). The rolls (QR) run from 1594 to 1972, when Quarter Sessions were
abolished and replaced by the Crown Courts.

Financial Records. These contain records of the county rate (QAF), the
accounts of the Treasurer, 1767–1829 (QAK), and rates for carriage
wages, and servants, 1755–1829 (QAR).

Roads and Bridges Records. Quarter Sessions had the power to hear
cases concerning bridges, and to make an assessment for their repair on
the inhabitants. Bridge records survive from 1617 to 1887 (QAB). Highway
diversions were enrolled on the Quarter Sessions Rolls.

Deposited Plans. A collection of plans of canals and river improvement,
piers, harbours and coastal work; turnpikes and other roads; bridges;
waterworks; houses of correction; railways; gas and electricity; and
boundary changes, 1792–1958 (QDP), which were required by statute to
be deposited with the Clerk of the Peace, from 1930, with the Clerks, and
since 1974, the Secretaries, of county councils. The deposited plans for
West Sussex (but note only for the area of the pre-April 1974 administrative county) are catalogued in Francis W. Steer, *A Catalogue of Sussex
Maps*, vol. 2, Sussex Record Society, vol. 66 (1968).

Electoral Records. These include the Land Tax Assessments, 1780–1832,
and Registers of Electors, 1832 to date (QDE).

Prison Records. These include formal minute books, reports, rules and
regulations, plans and miscellaneous records of the construction and
upkeep of Horsham Gaol, 1775–1846, and Petworth House of Correction,
1787–1880 (QAP).

Constabulary Records. These cover the establishment and expansion
of the County Police Force between 1839 and 1889 (QAC). Records of the
Worthing Borough Police Division, 1896–1957 (POL.W/W1), are also in
the Record Office.

Lunacy Records. These contain returns and reports of county and private asylums, 1842–1889 (QAL).

Religious Records. These include Sacramental Certificates, 1702–1802, (QDR/1), and Registration of Papists' Estates (QDR/5). There is a card index of the Returns of Dissenters Meeting Houses (QCR), which includes the material from the ecclesiastical records.

Records of Miscellaneous Associations. Registers of Charities, 1835–1912 (QDS/2); lists of Friendly Societies, 1804–1847 (QDS/3); returns of Savings Banks, 1817–1836 (QDS/4); and registers of Scientific and Literary Institutes, 1834–1864 (QDS/6).

Assize Records. The Assize Records are in the Public Record Office in London.

Petty Sessions Records. The records of the Petworth Petty Sessions and a few records of Horsham and Steyning have been deposited in the Record Office.

For further details, see Francis W. Steer (ed.), *A Descriptive Report on the Quarter Sessions, other Official and Ecclesiastical Records in the custody of the County Councils of West and East Sussex* (1954).

COUNTY COUNCIL RECORDS

These contain records of the West Sussex County Council and its committees from 1889 to date, and, more recently, the modern departmental records.

LIEUTENANCY AND MILITIA RECORDS

From Tudor times, lists were made periodically of those required to serve in the county's militia under the command of the lieutenant. Many of these muster rolls are preserved in the Public Record Office in London, but eighteen rolls for various parishes, 1620, 1621 (Add. MS. 2741) are in the West Sussex Record Office. County militia records for the period 1745–1915 are in the East Sussex Record Office, and are especially full for the Napoleonic period when additional private companies were raised. During the invasion scare of 1801 and 1803 parochial returns were made of livestock, transport vehicles, corn mills etc., and copies of some of these are in the parish records. There are militia books among the Raper Archives (Raper MSS. 228, 229), covering the period 1780 to 1827, together with miscellaneous militia papers, and there is a mass of material among the records at Petworth House.

EPISCOPAL RECORDS

For a detailed catalogue of these records, see Francis W. Steer and Isabel M. Kirby (eds.), *The Records of the Bishop, Archdeacons and Former Exempt Jurisdictions* (1966).

Episcopal Registers and associated documents: The Episcopal Registers (Ep. I/1), 1397–1838, contain commissions to judges, admissions, institutions, collations, resignations and exchanges of benefices, and lists of persons ordained.

Instance Causes: The records of the instance courts correspond to civil cases. The acts were entered in the Instance Books (Ep. I/10), 1506–1798, and the evidence was recorded in the Deposition Books (Ep. I/11), 1557–1694. The detailed papers produced in court will be found in the Miscellaneous Court Papers (Ep. I/15), 16th century–1850.

Detection Causes and Visitations: Proceedings in detection causes which correspond to criminal cases were generally begun by presentments at visitations. The causes are entered in Detection Books (Ep. I/17), 1538–1853. Incumbents, curates and churchwardens were compelled to attend visitations, when Libri Cleri (Ep. I/18), 1521–1893, were compiled, and to produce their titles from which Registers of Orders (Ep. I/19), 1582–1675, were compiled. Visitation Papers (Ep. I/20), survive from 1554–1910. Procurations (Ep. I/21), 1681–1901, were the fees payable by all benefices at visitations.

Churchwardens' Presentments (Ep. I/22), 1573–1917, were sometimes copied into Registers of Presentments (Ep. I/23), 1571–1682. Parish Register Transcripts (Ep. I/24), 1567–1936, and Church Terriers (Ep. I/25), 1572–1692, were collected at visitations. Church Inspections (Ep. I/26), 1602–1724, were really visitations and noted defects in the buildings.

Probate Records: Until 1857 wills were proved and administrations granted in the consistory court or in the peculiar courts of the Dean of Chichester and the Archbishop of Canterbury. These wills and administrations have been indexed up to 1800 by the *British Records Society*, vols. 49 and 64 (1915 and 1940). The Registers of Wills (STCI) commence in 1479. The wills of the wealthier members of society will be found in the Public Record Office. Probate Inventories (Ep. I/29), 1560–1834, including all jurisdictions, are indexed by persons and places in the card index in the Search Room. The 25,000 inventories are now being recatalogued and a printed catalogue is being prepared. A much smaller collection has survived for the Archdeaconry of Lewes, much of which since 1974 is in West Sussex; the records, however, are still in the East Sussex Record Office.

Other Episcopal Records: Marriage licences (Ep. I/9) and bonds, date from the sixteenth century, and indexes up to 1860 have been published by the *Sussex Record Society*, vols. 9, 12, 32 and 35. Faculty Papers (Ep. I/40), 1577–1861, include petitions, citations, estimates and plans. A faculty had to be obtained before the fabric of the church could be altered in any way. Church Building Papers (Ep. I/41), 1743–1935, are similar. Registers of Non-Resident Clergy (Ep. I/42), 1745–1885; Valors (Ep. I/44), 1582–1811; Convocation Papers, 1557–1919, and miscellaneous records which have strayed from other groups.

Manorial Records: The records of the episcopal manors include Cartularies (Ep. VI/I), thirteenth and sixteenth century; Rentals (Ep. VI/2), 1552–1894; Account Books (Ep. VI/4), 1521–1871, and the records of the individual manors.

Records of the Exempt Jurisdictions: The records of the Dean of Chichester's Peculiar (Ep. III) and the Exempt Deanery of Pagham and Tarring (Ep. IV) follow the same general pattern except that the Instance and Detection causes are both found in the Act Books.

CAPITULAR RECORDS

For a detailed catalogue of these records see Francis W. Steer and Isabel M. Kirby (eds.), *A Catalogue of the Records of the Dean and Chapter, Vicars Choral, St. Mary's Hospital, Colleges and Schools* (1967).

Dean and Chapter Records: These include statutes (Cap. I/2), 1534–1798; Act Books (Cap. I/3), 1472–1876; Episcopal Election Papers (Cap. I/6), 1560–1870; Installation Papers (Cap. I/8, 9), 1554–1850; Chapter Papers (Cap. I/10), 1530–1882; Bishop Sherburne's Foundations, Donations and Charters (Cap. I/13–16), 1520–1536; Deeds (Cap. I/17), 689–1674, see Alison M. Edwards, *Ancient Charters of the Dean and Chapter of Chichester, 689–1674* (1972); and Communars Accounts (Cap. I/23, 24), 1513–1901. The manorial and estate records include Rentals (Cap. I/26), 1521–1870; Registers of Leases (Cap. I/27), 1548–1859; Surveys (Cap. I/29), 1616–1856 and the records of the individual capitular manors, together with the records of the manors of the Dean, the Chancellor, the Precentor, the Treasurer and the Prebendaries (Cap. II).

Corporation of Vicars Choral Records: These include Charters and Statutes (Cap. III/I), 1467–1865; Act Books (Cap. III/2), 1731–1923; Registers of Leases (Cap. III/3A), 1692–1864, and other manorial and estate records.

The Records of St. Mary's Hospital: A similar series, with Account Rolls (Cap. IV/2) dating from 1549, and Leases (Cap. IV/3) from 1667.

Records relating to Colleges and Schools: Records of Grey Coat School, 1710–1840, Bishop Otter's College, 1848–1868, both in Chichester, and Chichester Theological College, 1840–1854.

Miscellaneous Records: Records of Cathedral services, including Cathedral music (Cap. VI/I) 1650–1780, and records of the Ecclesiastical Commissioners.

(The reader's attention is drawn to the Dunkin Collection in the British Museum (Add. MSS. 39326–39546) which consists of 221 volumes, compiled from many sources including the episcopal and capitular records relating mainly to Sussex clergy and families, and invaluable for the study of Sussex ecclesiastical records.)

PARISH RECORDS

The parish, though ecclesiastical in origin, was used from Tudor times as a unit of local secular administration. Civil parishes were created in 1894 and took over the purely civil functions of the old administration. Their boundaries may not coincide with those of the ecclesiastical parish.

Parish Registers: Besides the entries of baptisms, marriages and burials which give information for genealogy, population changes and public health, registers occasionally contain more miscellaneous material— parochial taxation lists, perambulations of parish boundaries, protestation returns, briefs (charitable collections) and political commentary. From 1754 the parties to a marriage were required to sign or mark the register, a useful gauge of literacy. A copy of parish register entries was forwarded annually to the bishop's registry at Chichester, and these Bishops' Transcripts for both East and West Sussex are available in the Record Office.

See *A Handlist of the Bishops' Transcripts, 1567–1936* (1970), and *Handlist of Parish Registers, Bishops' Transcripts and Modern Transcripts in the Diocesan Record Office* (1972).

Registers of banns, and registers of preachers and services will also be found.

Other records of the Incumbent: These are likely to include institutions, inductions and licences, faculties together with plans and contracts, and also glebe terriers, tithe books and other documents relating to income.

Overseers' Records: The accounts of the overseers of the poor list payments for outdoor relief to paupers, and the rate books those who paid the poor rate. Other overseers' records relate to settlement, apprenticeship and bastardy.

Other parish records: Parish rate and account books, both ecclesiastical and civil, contain lists of the more affluent inhabitants and details of expenditure, prices and wages; churchwardens' accounts often include references to changes in liturgy and ceremonial and repairs to fabric; vestry minutes often contain the debates which preceded the final decision to sanction parochial expenditure; surveyors of highway accounts show expenditure on the repair of roads and bridges. Records of parish charities, church schools, and material relating to tithes and inclosure, will also be found.

Modern parish records: These include minutes and accounts of the Parochial Church Council, and records of the Parish Meeting and the Parish Council.

A typescript catalogue of parish records arranged in alphabetical order of parishes is available in the Search Room. A comprehensive catalogue of all records, whether deposited or not, is being prepared for parishes within the 'new' West Sussex formed in 1974.

ROMAN CATHOLIC AND NONCONFORMIST RECORDS

ROMAN CATHOLIC RECORDS

Roman Catholic registers are usually kept in the local church and only a few date from the eighteenth century. The registers of the domestic chapels at Arundel Castle, Burton Park, Cowdray and Slindon House have been printed by the *Catholic Record Society*. An idea of the incidence of catholicism may be obtained from:—

1. Churchwardens' Presentments (Ep. I/22) of recusants and the resultant ecclesiastical action recorded in the Detection Books (Ep. I/17) and the miscellaneous court papers (Ep. I/15). A Register of Presentments, 1621–1626, 1628, 1664–1670 has been printed in *Sussex Record Society*, vol. 49.

2. Ecclesiastical Returns of adult recusants and recusant families in 1580 (Ep. I/37/1), 1593 (Ep. I/37/2) and 1727 (Ep. I/37/3) and also the Compton Census of 1676 (*Sussex Archaeological Collections*, vol. 45), Bishop Bowers' Visitation of 1724 (Ep. I/26/3), and the House of Lords Returns of 1767.

3. Quarter Sessions Rolls and Indictment Books, which, especially in the seventeenth century, contain lists of recusants and indictments for refusal to attend church.

4. Registration required by the Court of Quarter Sessions or the Clerk of the Peace. Catholic Oath Roll, 1778–1862 (QDR/7); Registers of Papists' Estates, 1717–1727 (QDR/5), and a certificate of convictions of Papists, 1744 (QDR/W6).

5. The Recusant Rolls of the Exchequer, 1592–1691, which are annual rolls of sheriffs' accounts relating to recusants' fines and forfeitures are preserved at the Public Record Office (E 377/1–82).

PROTESTANT NONCONFORMITY

The older Nonconformist registers begin in the 18th century, and many of these are preserved in the Public Record Office. A list of these is available in the Search Room at the West Sussex Record Office. For the seventeenth century, the ecclesiastical communicants' returns, the Quarter Sessions Rolls and the Indictment Books give parochial totals of dissenters and lists of conventicles and those attending them. Official county records, including registers of Dissenting Ministers, 1689–1832, registers of Quakers, 1716–1753, 1855, and the register of dissenters' places of worship, 1829–1853, are in the East Sussex Record Office at Lewes.

Methodist Records—the records of the Chichester Circuit, covering Barnham, Bognor, Chichester, Emsworth, Felpham, Littlehampton, Nutbourne, Nyetimber, Rustington, Selsey and Walderton, 1815–1958, have been deposited at the West Sussex Record Office, while the records of the Worthing Circuit are in the custody of Mr. C. E. Virgoe, 193 Dominion Road, Worthing. Some records will be found at the Methodist Archives and Research Centre, Epworth House, 25–35 City Road, London EC1Y 1AA.

Quaker Records—the records covering the whole county are deposited in the East Sussex Record Office at Lewes; a typescript catalogue is available in the Search Room at the West Sussex Record Office.

Other Denominations—records of the Ebenezer Chapel, Chichester, 1833–1857 (Add. MSS. 2425–2457); the Independent Chapel, Chichester, 1783–1892 (Add. MSS. 2458–2464); and the Chichester Congregational Church, 1892–1942 (Add. MSS. 2465–2541) are available in the West Sussex Record Office.

Addresses of religious repositories and libraries can be found in *Record Repositories of Great Britain* (5th edn., 1973) published by the Historical Manuscripts Commission.

BOROUGH RECORDS

The Corporation records of **Arundel** are at Arundel Town Hall and a typescript catalogue of them is available in the West Sussex Record Office. Some of the records are in the custody of Messrs. Holmes, Campbell and Co., solicitors of Arundel.

The records of **Chichester** are now in the Record Office and are described in F. H. W. Sheppard (ed.), *A Descriptive list of the Archives of the City of Chichester* (1949). There is also a typescript list of later records (1970).

Horsham was a manorial borough, and some of the records are in the Horsham Museum collection, a typescript catalogue of which is available in the West Sussex Record Office.

The **Midhurst** Borough records were deposited in the Record Office among the Cowdray Archives, and are catalogued in A. A. Dibben (ed.), *Catalogue of the Cowdray Archives*, vol. 2 (1964), pp. 189–381.

Steyning, New Shoreham and **Bramber** were manorial boroughs belonging to the Duke of Norfolk, and there are no records of these boroughs, or for **East Grinsted,** in the Record Office. The records of the Corporation of **Worthing** are at Worthing Town Hall.

DISTRICT COUNCIL RECORDS

Lists of their Minute Books, both Council and Committees, are held at the West Sussex Record Office and at the offices of each of the new Councils. As a result of Local Government re-organisation in 1974, in certain cases (e.g. Midhurst, Petworth, East Grinstead, Chichester R.D.C.) the Minute Books earlier than *c.*1933 have been deposited in the West Sussex Record Office.

In addition there have been some deposits of other records, *viz*: Medical Officer of Health and Public Health Inspector's Journals and Housing Ledgers (Chichester City); Treasurer's Ledgers and Rate Books (Chichester R.D.C.); Rural and Sanitary Authority Rate Books and Ledgers (Horsham R.D.C.); Highway Board Minute Books and Rate Books (Chichester R.D.C.).

POOR LAW AND WELFARE RECORDS

Prior to 1834, responsibility for the administration of poor relief lay with the parochial overseers, answerable to the Justices of the Peace in Quarter Sessions. The documents accumulated by the parochial overseers will be found among the parish records. Returns showing poor rate expenditure by parish between 1800 and 1817 are among the Quarter Sessions Records in the East Sussex Record Office.

The Poor Law Amendment Act of 1834 created unions of parishes each with a workhouse, administered by elected boards of guardians accountable to the Poor Law Commissioners. The minutes, ledgers, letter books, etc. of all the unions established in West Sussex are available in the Record Office. For details of these see Jane M. Coleman, *Sussex Poor Law Records* (1960). They illustrate many facets of workhouse administration such as diet, medical treatment, employment and education. Local union activity was often initiated by orders from the Poor Law Commissioners, which are in the Public Record Office. Some orders from 1834–1878 are also preserved among the Quarter Sessions records (QDS/1).

EDUCATION RECORDS

Charity Schools and Endowed Grammar Schools

Such institutions were normally endowed by the founder with property held by trustees responsible for ensuring that the curriculum and administration accorded with the founder's wishes. The records, therefore, often contain the will of the founder, the patent of foundation, minutes and account books of trustees, lists of scholars, etc. Many of these institutions are described in the *Victoria County History*, vol. 2 (1907), pp. 397–440. Episcopal licences granted to teachers in such schools can be found for the period up to the mid-eighteenth century among the ecclesiastical archives.

Voluntary Schools

The spread of sectarian education taught in voluntary schools built and maintained by Anglicans or Nonconformists, was particularly stimulated by the foundation of the National Society in 1811 and the British and Foreign School Society in 1814. West Sussex had a strong and early Anglican tradition and a strong Catholic tradition, but there are hardly any British Schools. The records of many such schools are available in the Record Office, and are particularly comprehensive when the minutes, correspondence and accounts of the managers are supplemented by the log books giving details of curriculum, discipline, equipment and amenities, outings and absences, and the attendance registers.

Board Schools

From 1870 Forster's Act set up, in areas insufficiently provided with voluntary schools, public elementary schools, built and maintained from local rates and administered by elected boards responsible through an inspectorate to the Board of Education. Attendance was eventually made compulsory and free. Thirty-one school boards were formed in West Sussex, and about half of these have left teachers' records, although only nine have left administrative records.

Local Education Authorities

In 1902 the local education authority suspended the school board. West Sussex County Council became the local education authority for the whole county. The Borough of Worthing, however, had its own education administration until 1974.

Mechanics' Institutes

Only records of the Chichester Mechanics' Institute, 1831–1924 (Add. MSS. 2849–2852) have so far been deposited in the Record Office. For details see Francis W. Steer, *The Chichester Literary and Philosophical Society and Mechanics' Institute, 1831–1924* (Chichester Paper no. 29, 1962).

HIGHWAY RECORDS

A variety of authorities have been responsible for the maintenance of roads:

The Justices in Quarter Sessions

Parochial responsibility for the upkeep of roads was defined in the mid-sixteenth century, surveyors of highways being elected to organise labour for maintenance (see Parish Records). The Justices of the Peace were responsible for ensuring that the parishes performed this duty effectively, and from 1733 they also authorised the diversion or closure of highways. From 1531 too, an increasing number of bridges were maintained from a county rate levied at Quarter Sessions.

Turnpike Trusts

From the eighteenth century onwards, responsibility for the maintenance, improvement or realignment of long stretches of major roads was vested by Act of Parliament in turnpike trusts. These were required to deposit plans with the Clerk of the Peace (for details see Francis W. Steer, *A Catalogue of Sussex Maps*, vol. 2 (1968), Sussex Record Society, vol. 66), and to supply, periodically, details of income and expenditure, tollhouse sites, etc. The local records of a turnpike trust may include acts, deeds, minute books, accounts, correspondence and contracts for building roads and tollhouses. Records of the following trusts are in the West Sussex Record Office: Storrington to Balls Hut (Add. MSS. 2109–2111); Stopham Bridge, Pulborough to Steyning (Add. MSS. 2112–2115); Marehill, Pulborough to Southwater (Add. MSS. 2116–2117); Petworth Turnpike Trust (Add. MS. 2212, see *Sussex Archaeological Collections*, vol. 95, pp. 105–115); Cowfold to Henfield (Add. MSS. 9148–9245); Horsham, Steyning and Beeding (Add. MS. 11,692); and Arundel to Bury and Fittleworth (Acc. 2706). Records of the Five Oaks Turnpike are at Petworth House.

Improvement Commissioners

These were responsible by Act of Parliament from the 18th century onwards for road maintenance in corporate towns. The minutes of the Worthing Commissioners are at Worthing Library and those of Chichester are in the West Sussex Record Office.

Later Highway Authorities

In the nineteenth century parochial responsibility for road maintenance was subjected to a succession of changes. In towns it passed to the Urban Sanitary Authorities from 1848 onwards, to Borough and Urban District Councils in 1894, and to the County Council in 1974. In rural areas it passed to Highway Boards from 1862 onwards, to Rural Sanitary Authorities from 1872 onwards, the main roads to the County Council in 1888, the secondary roads to Rural District Councils in 1894 and to the County Council in 1929.

RAILWAY RECORDS

The records of railway companies whose lines ran into West Sussex are preserved at the British Transport Historical Records Office in London. Records deposited in the West Sussex Record Office include Deposited Plans (see this handbook, p. 40 and Francis W. Steer, *A Catalogue of Sussex Maps*, vol. 2 (1968)); papers relating to the construction of the London, Brighton and South Coast Railway (Ep. VI/59); and papers relating to the Selsey Tramway (Raper MSS.). Miscellaneous records relating to land purchase by companies, and investment in the companies by individuals, can be found in various collections in the Record Office.

LAND DRAINAGE RECORDS

The land drainage records deposited in the Record Office include those of the Commissioners of Sewers for South West Sussex, 1687–1939, for the Rape of Arundel, 1726–1933, and for the Rape of Bramber, 1812–1933. The records of the three Catchment Boards which took over the powers of the Sewers Commissioners, 1930–1950, are also here. The Catchment Boards were succeeded by the West Sussex River Board in 1950, which in turn was succeeded by the Sussex River Authority in 1965. For details, see David J. Butler, *The Land Drainage Records of West Sussex* (1973).

INLAND NAVIGATION RECORDS
There are records of the River Arun Navigation, 1785–1894, and the River Adur Navigation, 1853–1890.

Miscellaneous records relating to canals will be found in various collections in the Office. Particular note should be taken of the Deposited Plans, and of the records of the 3rd Earl of Egremont at Petworth House relating to the Rother Navigation. A typescript catalogue of inland navigation records has been prepared, and will be published shortly.

HARBOUR COMMISSIONERS AND COASTAL SHIPPING RECORDS
The major source for the volume, direction and character of coastal and overseas trade from and to the West Sussex ports and for the tonnage and identity of the shipping involved, are the Port Books which date from the 1560s to the mid eighteenth century, in the Public Record Office in London. The State Papers also contain returns of shipping.

Some of the records of Shoreham Harbour Commissioners, 1760–1926, are deposited in the West Sussex Record Office. The records of Little-hampton Harbour Commissioners are with Messrs. Holmes, Campbell and Co., solicitors at Littlehampton, but a microfilm of the minute books is in the West Sussex Record Office. Typescript lists of both these collections are available in the Search Room at the Record Office. A list of ships registered in Arundel, Chichester, Littlehampton and Shoreham, 1822–1913, and the official returns of ships registered in these ports, 1863–1913, are in the Office. The Sussex Vice-Admiralty Court Papers, 1638–1688, are to be found among the ecclesiastical archives (Ep. I/55).

TAXATION RECORDS
These may be used with caution to determine the distribution of taxable wealth and population.

Lay Subsidies
These medieval taxations of movable property are in the Public Record Office. Those levied in Sussex in 1296, 1327 and 1332 have been published as *Sussex Record Society*, vol. 10. The more comprehensive taxation on land, movables or wages collected in 1524 and 1525 is printed in *Sussex Record Society*, vol. 50.

Hearth Tax
The returns for West Sussex are in the Public Record Office.

Land Tax
These returns, deposited in the West Sussex Record Office, list annually by parish the proprietors and occupiers of land and its rental value, and date from 1780 to 1832.

Parochial Rates
These are found among the parish records in the West Sussex Record Office.

MANORIAL AND ESTATE RECORDS

GENERAL

In the medieval period the manor was normally the unit of farm management and accountancy, but from the 16th century manorial records are increasingly supplemented by other estate documentation. A card index of all the manorial documents in the Record Office is available in the Search Room.

Details of Sussex manorial records not in the custody of the Record Office may be obtained from the Manorial Register at the National Register of Archives at Quality House, Quality Court, Chancery Lane, London, WC2A 1HP.

Manorial Court Rolls

These record the widely varied transactions in the manor court, transfers or inheritance of property, piecemeal inclosure of waste, encroachments, regulation of the communal farming routine and restatements of custom.

Manorial and Estate Accounts

These may yield evidence of expenditure on seed and livestock, wages, transport and materials and capital equipment and income from grain, livestock and timber sales, and occasionally from industrial activity such as ironworks and brickmaking. Grain accounts on the dorse of manorial accounts and crop books are of especial value for crop rotations and yield.

Title Deeds

These define the ownership and extent of property and provide information for the study of topography, genealogy and place names. Maps are sometimes drawn on the deeds. Marriage settlements often mirror the build up of estates.

Other Estate Records

These may include rentals, surveys, tenancy agreements and leases, sales particulars, estate correspondence and maps.

Household and Personal Papers

Often included among estate records are household accounts and personal correspondence, diaries and legal and official papers accumulated by holders of public office.

MANORIAL AND ESTATE COLLECTIONS IN THE WEST SUSSEX RECORD OFFICE

The Bosham Manor Records

Records of the estate of the Berkeley family centred on Bosham, Chidham and Funtington. They include a fine series of 14th century manorial accounts. A schedule is available in the Search Room of the Record Office.

The Burrell Manuscripts

Records of the estates of the Burrell family of Knepp Castle, Shipley, in the north-eastern part of West Sussex. A list prepared by the National Register of Archives is available in the Search Room at the West Sussex Record Office.

The Clough and Butler Archives
Estate and family records of the two families, including property in Amberley, Warminghurst and North Wales. See John M. L. Booker (ed.), *The Clough and Butler Archives* (1965).

The Cowdray Archives
A large collection of manorial and estate records of the Browne family, Viscounts Montague, relating principally to the parishes of Bepton, Cocking, Easebourne, Fernhurst, Lodsworth and Midhurst, which includes the records of the Borough of Midhurst, and a fine collection of maps and the correspondence of the 6th Earl of Egmont. See A. A. Dibben (ed.), *The Cowdray Archives*, vol. 1 (1960), and vol. 2 (1964).

The Goodwood Archives
The estate records of the Dukes of Richmond, including manorial documents and title deeds (principally relating to Boxgrove, East Dean, Halnaker, East and Mid Lavant, Singleton and Charlton, Tangmere, Westhampnett and West Itchenor), maps (notably the surveys of Yeakell and Gardner), and estate administration papers (including the race course). See Francis W. Steer and J. E. Amanda Venables (eds.), *The Goodwood Estate Archives*, vol. 1 (1970), and vol. 2 (1972) Appendix I.

The Greatham Archives
A small collection of estate records of this small parish. See A. A. Dibben (ed.), *The Greatham Archives* (1962).

The Lavington Archives
Records of the estate of the Garton, Orme and Sargent families centred on the parishes of Graffham and Woolavington, including the Garton cartulary and a few documents connected with the iron industry. See Francis W. Steer (ed.), *The Lavington Archives* (1964).

The Lytton Manuscripts
Records of the Crabbett and Newbuildings estates of the Blunt family. See Noel H. Osborne (ed.), *The Lytton Manuscripts* (1967).

The Mitford Archives
Records of the Mitford estate centred on the family seat at Pitshill in Tillington, including travel diaries, records of commercial transport schemes, election papers, and the papers of various members of the family. See Francis W. Steer (ed.), *The Mitford Archives*, vol. 1 (1961), and vol. 2 (1970).

The Sergison Archives
Estate records of the Sergison family of Cuckfield Park.

The Shillinglee Archives
Records of the Turnour estates centred on Kirdford, including a fine series of seventeenth century letters. A typescript catalogue is available in the Search Room at the West Sussex Record Office.

The Slindon Archives
A collection of manorial and estate records of the Kempe family and the Earls of Newburgh centred on their estate in Slindon. A list prepared by

the National Register of Archives is available in the Search Room at the West Sussex Record Office.

The Uppark Archives
Records of the Uppark estate in Harting and of the Featherstonhaugh family. They include a large collection of title deeds of Essex, London and Middlesex. A catalogue is being prepared.

The Wakehurst Place Archives
Estate records of the Wakehurst Place estate in Ardingly, West Hoathly, Balcombe and Worth. A duplicated list is available in the Search Room at the West Sussex Record Office.

The West Dean Archives
Manorial and estate records of the Peachey family centred on their estate at West Dean. A manuscript catalogue is available in the Search Room of the West Sussex Record Office, and will be printed shortly.

The Wiston Archives
A remarkably complete collection of title deeds of the Goring family estates covering most of the parishes of the eastern half of West Sussex and the western half of East Sussex. The collection includes a fine series of fourteenth and fifteenth century court rolls and manorial accounts, and a number of maps. See John M. L. Booker, *The Wiston Archives* (1975).

MISCELLANEOUS COLLECTIONS IN THE WEST SUSSEX RECORD OFFICE
Solicitors' Collections
Important collections have been deposited in the Record Office by Messrs. Albery and Lucas of Midhurst (NRA. list available); Messrs. Holmes, Campbell and Co., of Arundel and Littlehampton (NRA. list available); Messrs. Oglethorpe and Anderson of Petworth (catalogue in preparation); and Messrs. Raper and Co., of Chichester (catalogue in active preparation).

Additional Manuscripts
This collection embraces all the smaller gifts and deposits of documents as distinct from the large family and estate collections or accumulations from solicitors' offices. It now (1975) includes 18,000 documents, is catalogued in 21 typescript volumes, and is indexed by persons, places, subjects and manors in the card indexes in the Search Room.

Miscellaneous Papers
A collection of more than a thousand items consisting of transcripts of documents, xerox copies, working papers etc., which is indexed in the Search Room card indexes. A typescript list is also available.

CORRESPONDENCE COLLECTIONS IN THE WEST SUSSEX RECORD OFFICE
The Badcock Lovell Papers
Correspondence of William Stanhope Badcock (Lovell) and his family, principally concerned with naval matters and including a series of fine letters relating to the Peninsular War. For a detailed catalogue of the

correspondence, see Add. MSS. 1344–1412. It is hoped that an edited transcript of the Peninsular War letters will be published soon.

The Cobden Papers

A collection of the correspondence of Richard Cobden, his family (in particular Jane Cobden Unwin, his daughter), and friends. See Francis W. Steer (ed.), *The Cobden Papers* (1964), and Patricia Gill (ed.), *The Cobden and Unwin Papers* (1967).

The Druitt Papers

Correspondence of Robert Druitt, a nineteenth century London physician and surgeon, and his family. Robert Druitt was interested in medicine, sanitation, public health, wine, temperance, and church music. See Nigel Wratten (ed.), *The Druit Papers* (to be published shortly).

The Goodwood Archives

The correspondence and the personal, cultural and political papers of the Dukes of Richmond and their families. See Francis W. Steer and J. E. Amanda Venables (eds.), *The Goodwood Estate Archives*, vol. 2 (1972). Two further volumes will be published shortly—the first will contain catalogues and indexes of the Royal Letters, 1586–1740; the letters of the 1st Marquess of Montrose, 1645/6; the correspondence of the Dukes of Gordon, 1677–1860; the letters to the 2nd Duke from the Duke of Newcastle and Henry Pelham, 1732–1750; and the papers of the 6th Duke of Richmond (1818–1903) as President of the Board of Trade, and later, leader of the Tory Party in the House of Lords. The second will contain a comprehensive index of the extensive correspondence of the 5th Duke of Richmond, 1820–1860.

The Hawkins Papers

The correspondence of John Hawkins, 1761–1841, relating, *inter alia*, to botany, minerology, geology, natural history, architecture, literature and politics. See Francis W. Steer (ed.), *The Hawkins Papers* (1962); *The Letters of John Hawkins and Samuel and Daniel Lysons, 1812–1830* (1966); and . . . *I Am My Dear Sir* (1959).

The Kempe Papers

The papers and correspondence of Sir Alfred Bray Kempe, 1849–1922, who was Secretary of the Royal Commission on Ecclesiastical Courts, Treasurer and Vice-President of the Royal Society, and a music lover. A list prepared by the National Register of Archives is available in the Search Room.

The Maxse Papers

The papers and correspondence of various members of the Maxse family, and, in particular, of Admiral Frederick Augustus Maxse, 1833–1900, and of Leopold Maxse, 1864–1932, editor of the *National Review*. See Francis W. Steer (ed.), *The Maxse Papers* (1964). A catalogue of Leopold Maxse's papers is being prepared; an application in writing is necessary before these papers can be made available.

The Shillinglee Archives

The correspondence of the Turnour family, 1569–1939, mostly concerning Sir Edward Turnour, 1617–1676, Speaker of the House of Commons, and Sir Edward Turnour, 1643–1721, M.P. for Orford. See John Holworthy's and Miss Shilton's 'Catalogue of Letters in the possession of Earl Winterton at Shillinglee Park' (1922), which is available in the Search Room, together with two volumes of typescript copies of many of the letters.

The Wilberforce Archives

Papers and correspondence of the Sargent, Denman and Wilberforce families, and Henry Manning. They include an important collection of letters from Manning to Samuel Wilberforce. See Francis W. Steer (ed.), *The Wilberforce Archives* (1966). Samuel Wilberforce's papers are in the Bodleian Library, Oxford.

ANTIQUARIAN COLLECTIONS IN THE WEST SUSSEX RECORD OFFICE

The Challen Papers

Pedigrees, notes and correspondence relating principally to Sussex families, compiled by W. H. Challen, and catalogued as MP. 511–674. See *Index to Sussex Pedigrees in the Challen Papers*, Lists and Indexes, no. 6 (1964).

The Comber Papers

John Comber's pedigrees of Sussex families, now bound in 28 manuscript volumes. Only three volumes—*Sussex Genealogies. Horsham Centre* (1931), *Ardingly Centre* (1932), and *Lewes Centre* (1933)—were published. Includes Comber's annotated copy of Berry's *Sussex Genealogies*. See Francis W. Steer (ed.), *The Comber Papers*, Lists and Indexes, no. 2 (1955).

Lindsay Fleming's Papers

A very full collection of transcripts of documents relating to Aldwick Hundred, 680–1900, from Lambeth Palace Library, the British Museum, the Public Record Office and elsewhere, catalogued as MP. 443–452. See Lindsay Fleming, *History of Pagham in Sussex*, 3 vols. (1949–50).

The Heron-Allen Papers

Edward Heron-Allen's notes for his history of Selsey together with newspaper cuttings, photographs, maps, and printed miscellanea relating to Selsey, 1906–1937, catalogued as MP. 93–98, 110–118, 121. See E. Heron-Allen, *Selsey Bill: historic and prehistoric* (1911).

The Kenyon Papers

G. H. Kenyon's working papers and transcripts of documents relating mostly to Kirdford and Petworth, and catalogued as MP. 3,128, 1002–1062. See G. H. Kenyon, 'Kirdford Inventories, 1611–1776', in *Sussex Archaeological Collections*, vol. 93 (1955), pp. 78–156; *Kirdford: Some Parish History* (1971); and 'Petworth Town and Trades, 1610–1760', in *Sussex Archaeological Collections*, vol. 96 (1958), pp. 35–107; vol. 98 (1960), pp. 71–117, and vol. 99 (1961), pp. 102–148.

Lady Mary Maxse's Papers

Extracts and transcripts of documents mainly from the Public Record Office, Petworth House and printed sources, relating to Fittleworth and surrounding parishes, catalogued as MP. 63–81. See Lady Mary Maxse, *The Story of Fittleworth* (1935).

The Newnham Papers

Transcripts and notes relating mainly to Billingshurst, chiefly from documents still in the parish chest, and catalogued as MP. 216–319.

COLLECTIONS NOT IN THE WEST SUSSEX RECORD OFFICE

Arundel Castle Archives
The records of the Dukes of Norfolk are preserved at Arundel Castle. See Francis W. Steer (ed.), *Arundel Castle Archives*, vol. 1 (1968), vol. 2 (1972), and *The Earl Marshal's Papers at Arundel Castle*, Harleian Society vols. 115, 116 (1964). Facilities for research at Arundel Castle are strictly limited, and enquiries should be addressed to the Archivist and Librarian to His Grace the Duke of Norfolk, at Arundel Castle.

Petworth House Archives
The records of the Percy and Wyndham families are preserved at Petworth House. See Francis W. Steer and Noel H. Osborne, *Petworth House Archives*, vol. 1 (1968). Further catalogues are being prepared. Enquiries should be addressed to the County Archivist, West Sussex Record Office, Chichester. Documents may be consulted only at the Record Office and provided at least one week's notice is given.

Bognor Regis College of Education Library
Contains the Gerard Young Collection of books, postcards, drawings and printed ephemera etc. relating to Bognor Regis and surrounding villages. Prior application to the Librarian is essential.

British Library. Department of Manuscripts
Apart from the Burrell MSS., the Caryll MSS., and the Dunkin collection (qv.), the Harleian MSS., the Hayley MSS. and the Newcastle Papers (the latter both in Add. MSS.) contain much Sussex material. A reader's ticket must be obtained. See T. C. Skeat, *Catalogues of the Manuscript Collections in the British Museum* (1962).

Bodleian Library, Oxford
For details of Sussex material, see Phillipa Revill, *Handlist of Manuscripts relating to Sussex in the Bodleian Library, Oxford* (1957).[1]

The Burrell Manuscripts
The fifteen manuscript volumes prepared by Sir William Burrell, 1732–1796, for his projected history of the county, together with eight volumes of topographical drawings by Grimm, Lambert and others, are preserved in the British Library. The topographical drawings are on microfilm at the West Sussex Record Office, and some are published in Walter H. Godfrey and L. F. Salzman (eds.), *Sussex Views selected from the Burrell Collections* (1951). The collection also contains many original manuscripts, which are being microfilmed for the Record Office.

The Caryll Manuscripts
The records of the Caryll family and their estates, centred on Harting and West Grinstead, are preserved in the British Library (Add. MSS. 28,234–28,254). They also include the correspondence of John Caryll as secretary to Queen Mary of Modena, and a series of letters from Alexander Pope.

Christ's Hospital Archives
Founded in 1552 in Newgate Street, London, Christ's Hospital moved to Sussex in 1902, together with some of the school's archives and antiquities.

---

[1] This catalogue does not include Samuel Wilberforce's papers mentioned on p. 58 above, or those of Thomas Sanctuary relating to the 1830 riots in Horsham.

The bulk of the administrative archives of the Hospital are now to be found either in the Guildhall Library or at the School's London Office at 26 Great Tower Street, but there is at Horsham documentary material of a literary as well as an administrative nature. There is also a collection of portraits, prints and early photographs, and general scholastic ephemera dating back to early times.

The Danny Archives
Records of the Goring, Campion and Courthope families. Estate archives centred on Danny, Cuckfield, Hurstpierpoint and Lewes. The personal and official papers include some relating to the Civil War and to the Indian Mutiny. See Judith A. Wooldridge, *The Danny Archives* (1966). This collection is in the East Sussex Record Office at Lewes.

The Hickstead Place Archives
The records of the Stapley, Wood and Davidson families of Hickstead Place, Twineham, consist mainly of title deeds and estate papers relating to Twineham, Hurstpierpoint and Keymer. They include a fine series of farming account books dating from 1642. The collection is in the East Sussex Record Office at Lewes. See Judith A. Brent, *The Hickstead Place Archives* (1975).

The Horsham Museum Collection
A miscellaneous collection of documents relating to Horsham and its surrounding area are preserved at the Museum. They contain the Albery Papers and those of Thomas Medwin, a local solicitor. A typescript catalogue of some of the records is available in the Search Room at the West Sussex Record Office. It is hoped that a comprehensive catalogue will eventually be prepared and printed.

The Public Record Office
This houses the official records of the central organs of administration. There is thus Sussex material in almost every collection. See M. S. Giuseppi, *Guide to the Contents of the Public Record Office*, 3 vols. (1963–8). A reader's ticket must be obtained.

Sussex Archaeological Society
A number of collections of records relating to West Sussex have been deposited with the Sussex Archaeological Society. Details are given in K. W. Dickins, 'The Muniments of the Sussex Archaeological Trust: Guide to the Calendars', in *Sussex Archaeological Collections*, vol. 93 (1955), pp. 171–200. There are also several important collections of working papers of antiquarians, archaeologists and historians relating to their Sussex researches. These include the papers of A. Hadrian Allcroft (prehistoric and Roman earthworks); Henry de Candole (Henfield); E. Cecil Curwen (prehistoric archaeology); L. V. Grinsell (barrows); O. H. Leaney (church architecture); G. D. Johnston (bridges and rivers); L. F. Salzman (papers concerning his editorship of the Sussex Volumes of the *Victoria County History*); F. Bentham Stevens (visitations and archdeaconry returns, paper mills and moated sites); and Ernest Straker (Wealden iron industry, moated sites, turnpikes and Ashdown Forest). The collection, which, at present, continues to be housed at the Society's headquarters at Barbican House, Lewes, is administered by the East Sussex Record Office, Pelham

House, Lewes. Documents are normally produced at the Record Office on at least one day's notice.

The Papers of Viscountess Wolseley

This collection deposited in Hove Public Library includes the military papers of Field Marshall Lord Wolseley (1833–1913) and papers relating to Sussex local history and buildings, horticulture and the personal interests of Viscountess Wolseley (1872–1936). A list prepared by the National Register of Archives is available in the West Sussex Record Office.

PRINTED BY MOORE AND TILLYER AT THE REGNUM PRESS, CHICHESTER

PUBLICATIONS OF THE WEST SUSSEX RECORD OFFICE

*A HANDLIST OF SUSSEX INCLOSURE ACTS AND AWARDS. (Reprinted from *Sussex Archaeological Collections*, vol. 88, 1950) Pp. iv+48. Manilla covers.

A DESCRIPTIVE REPORT ON THE QUARTER SESSIONS, OTHER OFFICIAL AND ECCLESIASTICAL RECORDS IN THE CUSTODY OF THE COUNTY COUNCILS OF EAST AND WEST SUSSEX. 1954. Pp. xii+212. Manilla covers. 75p.

*A CATALOGUE OF SUSSEX POOR LAW RECORDS. 1960. Pp. xxix+72; 9 plates. Full cloth.

THE CROOKSHANK COLLECTION [of books]. 1960. Pp. xxii+41; 5 plates. Full cloth. 80p.

*THE COWDRAY ARCHIVES, Part I. 1960. Pp. xxxviii+187; 9 plates; pedigree. Full cloth. £2.

THE COWDRAY ARCHIVES, Part II. 1964. Pp. 234. Full cloth. £3.50.

THE MITFORD ARCHIVES, [Vol. I]. 1961. Pp. xi+83; 9 plates; pedigree. Full cloth. £1.25.

THE MITFORD ARCHIVES, Vol. II. 1970. Pp. vii+67. Full cloth. £3.

THE GREATHAM ARCHIVES. 1962. Pp. xviii+22. Manilla covers. 50p.

A CATALOGUE OF SUSSEX ESTATE AND TITHE AWARD MAPS. (Sussex Record Society, vol. 61, 1962.) Pp. xvi+240. Full cloth. £2.50.

*A CATALOGUE OF SUSSEX MAPS. (Sussex Record Society, vol. 66, 1968.) Pp. vi+228. Full cloth.

THE HAWKINS PAPERS. 1962. Pp. viii+36; 1 plate; pedigree. Manilla covers. 75p.

THE LETTERS OF JOHN HAWKINS AND SAMUEL AND DANIEL LYSONS, 1812–1830. 1966. Pp. xvi+82; 5 plates. Full cloth. £2.

THE MAXSE PAPERS. 1964. Pp. viii+36. Manilla covers. 95p.

THE LAVINGTON ESTATE ARCHIVES. 1964. Pp. xii+128; 5 plates; pedigree. Full cloth. £2.

*THE COBDEN PAPERS. 1964. Pp. xii+126; 5 plates; pedigree. Full cloth.

THE COBDEN AND UNWIN PAPERS. 1967. Pp. v+50. Manilla covers. £1.75.

THE CLOUGH AND BUTLER ARCHIVES. 1965. Pp. x+56; 3 plates; pedigree. Manilla covers. £1.50.

THE WILBERFORCE ARCHIVES. 1966. Pp. v+33. Manilla covers £1.

THE RECORDS OF THE BISHOP, ARCHDEACONS AND FORMER EXEMPT JURISDICTIONS. 1966. Pp. xxiii+268. Full cloth. £4.75.

*THE RECORDS OF THE DEAN AND CHAPTER, VICARS CHORAL, ST. MARY'S HOSPITAL, COLLEGES AND SCHOOLS. 1967. Pp. xxiii+102. Full cloth.

A HANDLIST OF THE BISHOPS' TRANSCRIPTS, 1567–1936 [For the Diocese of Chichester.]. 1970. Pp. i+36. Manilla covers. 30p.

THE ERIC GILL MEMORIAL COLLECTION. 1967. Pp. iv+26. 4 plates. Manilla covers. 30p.

THE LYTTON MANUSCRIPTS. 1967. Pp. ix+79; 4 plates; pedigree. Full cloth. £2.75.

THE JOHN EDES HOUSE, WEST STREET, CHICHESTER. 1968. Pp. 15. 15 plates; pedigree. Manilla covers. 25p.

ARUNDEL CASTLE ARCHIVES. 12 handlists comprising the first volume. (Details supplied upon application to the West Sussex Record Office.)

ARUNDEL CASTLE ARCHIVES, Vol. II. 1972. Pp. vii+242. Full cloth. £7.50.

THE PETWORTH HOUSE ARCHIVES, Vol. I. 1968. Pp. xvi+207; 5 plates; pedigree. Full cloth. £6.

THE GOODWOOD ESTATE ARCHIVES, Vol. I. 1970. Pp. xxi + 309; 5 plates; pedigree. Full cloth. £7.25.

THE GOODWOOD ESTATE ARCHIVES, Vol. II. 1972. Pp. xx+168; 5 plates. Full cloth. £6.75.

QUARTER SESSIONS AND THE JUSTICES OF THE PEACE IN WEST SUS-SEX. 1972. Pp. 13. Paper covers. 20p.

THE TOWN PLANS OF CHICHESTER, 1595–1898. 1972. Pp. 27; 10 maps. Manilla covers. 50p.

TYPESCRIPT HANDLISTS. (Details supplied upon application to the West Sussex Record Office.)

THE LAND DRAINAGE RECORDS OF WEST SUSSEX. 1973. Pp. lx+177; 3 maps. Full cloth. £6.25.

RESTRICTED GRANDEUR: IMPRESSIONS OF CHICHESTER, 1586–1948. 1974. Pp. vi+57; 4 plates+27 line drawings. Manilla covers. 75p.

THE WISTON ARCHIVES. 1975. Pp. xiv+541; 5 plates; 2 pedigrees. Full cloth. £12.

LOCAL HISTORY IN WEST SUSSEX. A GUIDE TO SOURCES. 1975. Pp. v+61; 3 plates. Manilla covers. 2nd revised edn. 75p.

*Out of print in 1975   OTHER TITLES IN PREPARATION

Enquiries should be addressed to
THE COUNTY ARCHIVIST, WEST SUSSEX RECORD OFFICE
COUNTY HALL, CHICHESTER PO19 1RN   (Tel. Chichester [0243] 85100)

Tarosvanys

Six short tales for a long winter evening – you may not sleep afterwards!

According to Morton Nance's Cornish dictionary the word 'Tarosvanys'
means 'illusory, fantastic, unreal'. These stories, set in West Penwith,
will haunt your daytime thoughts.

Elaine Gill

Byth war !

Elaine Gill

PALORES PUBLICATIONS' 21st CENTURY WRITERS

Elaine Gill
Tarosvanys

ISBN 978-1-906845-18-6

Published by:

Palores Publications,
11a Penryn Street,
Redruth,
Cornwall.
TR15 2SP

Designed and printed by:

ImageSet,
63 Tehidy Road,
Camborne,
Cornwall.
TR14 8LJ
01209 712864

Typeset in Sabon 11/13pt

For All my Friends in the
'Turkey Rhubarb Band'/'Bagas Tavol Turkey'

Thanks to Laura for help with the cover

Contents

Tansys Montol – the Midwinter Bonfire   1

Boscawen-Un   6

Zacky and Wella   11

The Door   14

Once in a Blue Moon   17

An Dewhelans – The Return   21

Tansys Montol –
the Midwinter Bonfire

It is a perfect Penwith day of gold and blue and green. Sea, sky and gorse are at their best and brightest, as I sit here by the Jubilee Bathing Pool watching the rainbow flags of the Golowan Festival stirring in the light breeze. You may have heard of this festival that is held in Penzance each year at midsummer. We enjoy music, dancing and song, colour and laughter as we celebrate the longest day and the lightest time of the year. The week of celebration includes two significant days which we observe. The first is the Feast of St John the Baptist, whose head was presented on a plate at the request of Salome the dancing girl, and this unfortunate event is recalled as part of our town crest. And the second is the moment of the Summer Solstice. From this point on, as the wheel of the year turns, the light diminishes day by day until the midwinter festival of Montol is reached in December, at the darkest time of the year. And this is when my tale is set.

It is a murky, gloomy period when the body needs warmth, and the heart and spirits look for some comfort in fire and ale. In Cornwall, and in Penwith particularly, there is a tradition of 'guise' dancing and I belong to a band of musicians and dancers who try and mitigate the dreary darkness by marking the tipping of the balance and consequent return of the sun, or so we hope, at the Winter Solstice. The midwinter festival of Montol brings respite from the cold, dark days of winter. It introduces light and glitter to chase away the sadness and shadows and it marks a period of misrule, of chaos.

'Guise dancing' requires that we use some sort of disguise for our performance so, consequently, for the occasion we wear 'mock formal' attire which adds to the mystery and hidden nature of things at this season. Our black outfits are complemented by Venetian style eye-masks to disguise our features, with the aim of further confusing and disorientating the onlooker. People invest a lot of time and effort in making their own costumes and some of the masks are especially sinister and mysterious rendering the wearer totally unrecognisable. Another of our hallmarks is that our tunes are often deliberately hypnotic and funereal, once again reflecting the dismal weeks before the welcome return of the sun and its warmth. But to my story ...

That evening we gathered, as usual, in the congenial atmosphere of the 'Admiral Benbow' pub in Chapel Street and, after ample refreshment, made our way in stately procession through the darkening streets of the town towards the ancient site of Lescudjack hill-fort, situated high above the houses and shops. Playing tunes as we walked, I was conscious of the melodies echoing in the alleyways and reverberating from the stones and bricks as we passed. The light drizzle that had been dogging the afternoon had now stopped and although the sky over Mount's Bay was overcast and the sea dull and leaden, spirits were high and we were out to enjoy ourselves and to entertain and delight.

At the top of Castle Road we turned into the field where the Montol ceremony was to be held. The dim weather was in sharp contrast to the brilliant 'River of Fire' lanterns lighting up the night sky – swaying paper and flames, so different from the deep velvet darkness pressing in upon us. Soon the huge bonfire was ablaze, its tongues of fire leaping into the inky sky. Its offering of heat and light stirred in me primitive half-memories of ghostly wolves and bears that might well be waiting outside the ring of the firelight, but most people had no thought for anything other than enjoyment of the present moment and the beauty of the scene.

I play near the front of the band with the melody instruments and so it is sometimes difficult to see who else has turned up, especially as we often have visitors who join us just for one event, and of course we are all disguised. However, over the weeks I have become familiar with costumes and body-shapes and gaits so that I think I know all the regular members of the 'Turkey Rhubarb Band' now. Sometimes it is possible to tell whether certain members have arrived just by listening – the owners of the tuba and the triangle can be identified whether masked or not!

I passed my gaze over the assembled crowd. The eager faces of young children shone in the firelight as they watched the results of their labours, the yellow lanterns suspended high above their heads, illuminating the shadowy surroundings. Excitement ran high and infectious good spirits prevailed. There was no suggestion of anything ominous or threatening on that evening. We played, we danced, we sang, we gave thanks and implored whatever deity we respected and we begged the sun to return to us in due season.

During a lull in the proceedings I took time to admire the costumes of my fellow band members and guess which friend or acquaintance was hidden under flowing cloak, dinner jacket or black satin dress. Net, lace and feathers abounded, adding greatly to the sense of the occasion.

One person I did not know stood alone, a little behind the drummers to my left. He wore the customary black jacket complemented by a tall, black stove-pipe hat and white face-mask which glittered as though covered in hoar frost. Silver icicles hung from the rim of his battered hat. His mask gave him the look of an eerie skull which had not quite lost all its flesh, of a body that had been in the water for some time and was drained of its life-blood and colour.

Chalky-white and cold, he faced the red, gold and orange of the blazing fire before him with impassive countenance.

Despite his fearful face-mask he looked very impressive. The man and his costume intrigued me and I wanted to make contact with him. I was determined to engage him in conversation and so when the opportunity came I moved over to him and facing him, stuck out my hand, announcing my name. I looked straight into his eyes – only I couldn't see them because of the nature of his disguise and only two black eyeholes met my gaze. I shivered. His grip was like iron, rigid and cold. I found it hard to withdraw my frozen hand from his grasp. His rasping voice croaked back at me, "Mr de Winter, Ivan Bernard de Winter, at your service, ma'am." I hardly had time to acknowledge his quaint way of speech to myself before the band started playing the next tune and I returned quickly to my position near the front to join in.

The ceremony was nearing its end when the stranger in the tall hat and frosty mask very quickly moved forward and, without hesitation, walked straight into the towering conflagration. A communal gasp of horror escaped from the assembled crowd. A shocked silence fell. The soaring flames licked around his body and head and, as he turned to face us, his mask slipped sideways when one of the retaining bands burned away. Revealed was a face identical to the mask that had fallen off: a chalk-white, expressionless visage with two black, empty eye-sockets and a gaping mouth.

Within seconds this apparition had disappeared completely and the people in the crowd very quickly began to doubt what they thought they had seen only moments before. The 'Turkey Rhubarb Band' launched into the tune of 'Tansys Montol' and the gathering immediately recovered, laughing and chatting noisily. As far as I am aware, no-one spoke of the matter. I certainly didn't share thoughts with anyone about it. And now I'm not sure if it really happened as I thought it did ...

The months passed and spring gave way to the softness of summer. And here I am, sitting on the low wall of St Anthony's Gardens in the hot summer sunshine reflecting on the triumph over light over dark, of the sunlight over the bitter cold, and Mr I. B. de Winter ... and his amazing gift to us.

Boscawen-Un

She had always loved the way the tiny chips of mica gleamed in granite when it caught the light. It reminded her of a pair of silver party shoes that she had when she was eight, or how the frost glistened on the roof of the old garden shed at home on cold winter mornings. Home. This was home now. She had left her childhood home and the shed twenty-five years ago to go to college. Cornwall didn't boast of any further education facilities at that time, and so everyone had to leave the county if they wanted professional training. Jobs and marriage meant that she had lived on 'the wrong side of the Tamar' ever since. And now she had been back for a whole three weeks. She leaned her cheek against the granite wall beside the door and felt profoundly grateful.

This part of the county was relatively unknown to her. She had grown up on the other coast but had not thought it wise to return to the same place. Here she was, a quarter of a century and a lot of heartache later. Everything would have changed and moved on. Better start afresh somewhere new. And yet ... it was still home in a funny sort of way.

"I'm getting too sentimental," she thought, and went inside out of the fresh March breeze. She buttered some saffron cake and made herself a pot of Earl Grey tea in the small, tidy kitchen and took a tray through to the sitting room. The dogs stirred on the rug in front of the fire, one of them thumping his tail laconically on the wooden floor. There were still some cardboard boxes to unpack in this room, but she was in no hurry. There was no urgency. She was where she was meant to be, and would build her environment slowly and with care. She was home. Sitting on the chaise-longue in the window sipping the tea, she idly picked up a booklet and read, "At Boscawen-Un stone circle on the gloriously sunny afternoon of 21 September 1928, Pedrog, the Archdruid of Britain, assisted by a number of Ovates, Bards, and Druids of the Welsh Gorsedd, inaugurated the first Gorsedd of Cornwall". Boscawen-Un. Hadn't she seen that name on the map? Wasn't it quite near? She stretched over to a lower shelf and pulled out the local Ordnance Survey map. Yes, it was about two miles away. Or was it less? She couldn't really get the hang of these metric maps, having been used to the older 'one-inch' ones.

"Come on then, lads. Time for a walk!" At these words the dogs sprang into action, although moments before all had been tranquillity and perfect calm. Whippets were like that, quite cat-like most of the time, but immediately active when required to be so. She pulled on a thick woolly hat and Wellington boots, and a waxed coat as protection against the spring chill. Perhaps it was too late to go out, the sun was nearly setting?

The ground was surprisingly firm under foot after the long damp winter, and in places the hedgerows were still jewelled with the last rich, red berries of the hawthorn bushes which survived the wildness and ferocity of the winter gales by bending and growing with the prevailing wind. They leaned like old women stretching out their bony fingers to catch the hair of unwary walkers. Droplets of moisture hung on the few remaining bracken fronds. It was quite misty, and once a cow loomed unexpectedly close and startled her, although it was probably more frightened than she was. The dogs rooted and ran up and down the hedgerows excitedly, but surprisingly didn't stray too far despite all the wonderful new scents. The liquid mist made the silence seem profound.

It stopped sounds from travelling far; there was no late bird-song or comforting noise of distant human activity, no tractor engine or barking dog. She felt like a silk-worm in a cocoon as she tramped through the fields.

Boscawen-Un wasn't difficult to find. She felt drawn to it. It was almost as if the path led straight there, as if the silvery mist parted and made a tunnel for her to walk along. She chided herself for being fanciful, but the magnetic pull was almost tangible. At last the pale mist revealed a low circle of dark stones with a single leaning pillar near the centre. One particular stone caught her attention. It was paler than the others and its quartz gleamed softly in the fading light. She walked around the outer edge of the ring, and laying her left hand flat against its surface felt a warmth pass through her flesh.

She stepped forward, and as she entered the stone circle the transformation took place. Suddenly there was a soft golden light. Her arms were bare. She glanced down and saw that she was wearing a long tunic with a fine woollen cloak, pinned at the breast with a large, ornate metal brooch shaped like a hare. Her feet were enclosed in delicate leather, laced with thongs. She felt strong and alive. Without thinking, she raised her arm in a blessing as a Celtic high-priestess should, and each person bowed their head to receive it. It was Alban Eiler, the Spring Equinox, the time of sowing and new beginnings when light and dark are held perfectly in balance.

And then the scene faded as quickly as it had come. Her eyes now rested on a woman sitting at the base of one of the stones in meditation, wrapped in a blue plastic anorak and with a vacuum flask at her side. The figure rose rather stiffly after having sat still for so long, and as their eyes met the woman bowed deeply, then picking up her rucksack, turned and disappeared into the mist.

Now alone, she leaned against the central granite stone, feeling the coldness and dampness of it on her face. She had come home. Maybe fifteen hundred years later, but she had indeed come home. She did not visit Boscawen-Un again until the autumn. The experience in the spring had stirred up many memories in her. Not only had it earthed her and made her feel welcome in the land, but it had also unsettled her, and she wasn't sure that she wanted to bear the responsibility of its implications alone.

It was an idyllic afternoon in September when she made her way once more along the deep track to the stone circle. Six months ago new life had been springing everywhere in the mild climate of Penwith; fresh green shoots pouring forth like music and the first celandines appearing in the greening banks. Now the year had passed into maturity and its fullness was revealed. It was Alban Elved, the Autumn Equinox, when once again the light and the dark are balanced; and again Boscawen-Un was calling her, and she had to respond to its urgency.

At first she didn't notice the tall man standing to one side. She had already seated herself at the base of the quartz stone with the intention of sitting quietly for a while, but when she saw him she felt compelled to rise and move towards him. He wore an Aran jersey with interlacing knotwork and dark green corduroy trousers. His hair curled around his head like a soft halo, and despite his gentle appearance he had the look and nobility of a Celtic warrior. As she approached he held out his right hand and without hesitation she took it in her left. It felt so natural. He held her gaze for a long moment and it seemed to her that his face shifted and changed, and catching her breath, she experienced an instant of deep recognition. She had known this man for a very long time, through many lifetimes. He spoke slowly and quietly. "I am

Carow." She nodded. "I know," she said. That was all. There was nothing else to say. He held her close and she closed her eyes, laying her cheek against his rough woollen jersey. He spoke gently into her hair. "I cannot go with you beyond the circle for I am in my spirit body, but I will be here whenever you call." She pressed closer into his warmth and felt his arms folded around her.

"*Dynergh dhys tu ha tre,*"* he whispered softly. And she knew with her whole being that this was home.

*Welcome home

Zacky and Wella

"If you're my guardian angel then why don't you protect me from harm?" I asked. Zacky considered and smiled, turning up one corner of his mouth in an infuriating manner, and rippled one of his wings. I have never really believed he was called Zacky. Another of his jokes. "Because you have free will," he replied, far too easily. That was his answer to a lot of my questions. Totally unsatisfactory.

"Take that hot cup of tea that landed in my lap in the canteen at lunchtime and ruined my trousers," I asked. "What's free will got to do with that?"

"You chose to sit at that table. You chose to go to the canteen. You chose to go for the interview that got you the job at that office."

I could see I wasn't going to get very far. I know what you're thinking. Most people don't have guardian angels, let alone see and talk to them. Well, let me tell you, that's where you're wrong – about having them, I mean. Everybody has one, although I'll agree that most people don't communicate with them in quite the same way that I do with Zacky.

I've always been able to see him. When I was little, my mum and dad used to humour me about him and make a space for him at the meal-table, but when I got to the age when they thought that I shouldn't be having 'imaginary' friends anymore, they got quite cross. Then there came a time when I realised that no-one was going to believe me, and so I gave in and stopped trying to convince them.

So, what about this free-will thing, I thought; but I didn't think about it very much. I spent more time thinking about Tamsin. I had met her two months ago on the train home when I had offered her my seat. It seems we were both in the habit of catching the 5.18, and we also both liked to be in the first carriage. We met regularly after that, and not just on the train either.

This Friday evening was going to be special. Tamsin had taken this afternoon off work to have her hair done, and I was leaving an hour early to catch the 4.18 home. We were going up to Plymouth to see a show.

With a light heart I stepped into the lift. Between floors four and five it stopped. Just stopped. I couldn't believe it. I pressed every button in turn and cursed myself for not using the main lift at the other end of the corridor. I had reckoned this one would be quicker as it wasn't used much. I went through the whole gamut of emotions: annoyance, frustration, worry, fear, anger, total fury, and finally, plain misery. I looked at the hands on my wrist-watch moving slowly from 4.00 to 5.00 with disbelief. That was the end of me catching the 4.18 and having plenty of time to get ready without a rush.

Then quite suddenly and without any explanation the lift juddered and continued its downward journey as smoothly as if nothing was out of the ordinary. When it reached the ground floor there was no-one around to question or complain to, as everyone had already gone home except for the security guard on the outside gate.

I hurried along the slippery, wet pavements, pulling up my jacket collar against the damp, still feeling ruffled and angry. Just as I was nearing the railway station a double-decker bus pulled up, and on the spur of the moment I hopped on. It was three hundred yards less to walk in the wet, even though the bus took a bit longer.

As I opened my flat door I could hear the 'phone ringing.
I grabbed the receiver: it was Tamsin. She just kept saying, "Oh Wella, Oh Wella," and then burst into tears. It took quite a while to get the whole story. It seems that the front carriage of the 4.18 train had been derailed, and everyone in it seriously injured. I swallowed hard. "Oh Wella, it's made me realise how much I care. I really do." I swallowed again and glanced up. A small but perfect golden feather floated softly down and landed on the telephone directory beside my hand. "You want to thank your lucky stars," sobbed Tamsin. There was a silence. "Or my guardian angel," I breathed softly, staring hard at the feather.

The Door

At first I was not sure whether to tell you this story, but it happened over ten years ago now and time lends distance to difficult memories and strange events.

As you may know, we are fortunate in Penzance to have one of the oldest private libraries in the country: the Morrab Library standing in its exotic sub-tropical garden not far from the centre of the town. Palm trees and giant ferns flourish in this sheltered paradise and in the spring the magnolia blossoms lie like alabaster sculptures against the powder blue of the clear sky.

However, it is a warm day in early autumn when my story begins: Thursday 9th September 1999, to be precise. Keen for me to succeed at languages, my parents had engaged a tutor for me for two weeks during the school holidays. Initially I was excited at the prospect and imagined a glamorous young French woman. In reality Mlle. Anfusek was middle-aged, thin and pinched. Apparently she was alone in the world and my parents hinted that she had endured hardships and adversities although these were never specified. The experiences had certainly not sweetened her temper.

Today she had decided that we would visit the Morrab Library and see what delights Molière and Balzac could offer us. After making ourselves known to the librarian at the reception desk I trailed behind my tutor up the elegant central staircase. I had known this building since I was a toddler and had spent happy times here with both my father and my mother. It had given me a great love for books, but today I would much rather have been down in the surf at Gwenver on my body-board. We turned right at the top of the stairs and along a short corridor, then down a small flight of steps into the room where the theology and the foreign language books are kept. The room smelled pleasantly of beeswax polish.

My tutor enthusiastically ran her finger along the spines of the French books, pulling out one or two volumes and placing them on the small table by the window. I gazed out of the window and thought of Sennen Beach. Then her attention was drawn to a door in the corner of the room. It looked like all the other doors in the library – made of oak with fielded panels – except that this one had a circular wrought-iron handle and a small door-knocker in the shape of a monkey's head. I have to say that I had no recollection of seeing this door before, but then I hadn't ever spent much time in this particular room.

Mlle. Anfusek turned the handle eagerly and the door swung open with ease. But to me it didn't feel right. I'm not ashamed to tell you that I was scared and caught hold of Mlle. Anfusek's jacket to try and stop her entering. However, she was determined and as she pushed open the door it revealed a short well-lit corridor with another identical door at the end. My interest was now aroused and I followed and stood behind her as she turned the large, twisted iron ring that raised the latch of the second door. The monkey's-head door-knocker grinned.

Nothing could have prepared me for what lay beyond that door. A room, hexagonal in shape, shelves of ancient books lining the walls, glass cases of stuffed animals, strange pieces of scientific equipment that I could not name, a large globe of the world in a stand, and even a human skeleton suspended beside one of the bookcases. More books were piled up on the floor beside an enormous oak desk, ornately carved and decorated with the same monkeys' heads that we had seen on the door-knockers. And then we saw him. Sitting quietly at the leather-topped desk in one of the angles of the room was an elderly man dressed in rust-coloured velvet knickerbockers and jacket, a waterfall of lace at his throat. We both froze in horror, but he smiled at us and spoke kindly.

"Ah, my dears, I am so glad you have come. You see, I need someone to take my place here, to take up residence in this wonderful room. I have waited a long time for your visit; since Wednesday 8th August 1888, in fact."

I did some quick mental arithmetic; my mind lurched sideways. I managed to make my feet move back towards the door and just as it was swinging shut I squeezed through and fled back to the sanity of the room where we had so recently planned to look at the French language books. They were still lying on the table in the warm sunshine where Mlle. Anfusek had put them. I didn't stop but ran straight down the stairs and out into the fresh air of a September afternoon in 1999. Never had the Morrab Gardens looked so beautiful.

That afternoon several people at Penzance rail station were startled by an unusual passenger who boarded the train for London. He was dressed in rust-coloured velvet knickerbockers and jacket, buckled shoes and a tall black hat, a waterfall of lace at his throat. He carried a Malacca cane with a monkey's-head handle.

Some years later when I summoned enough courage to return to that awful room, as I had half-expected, there was no longer a door in that wall.

As for Mlle. Anfusek – she was never seen again.

Once in a Blue Moon

"Wish they'd all go 'ome. I do honest. Fed up wi' them, I am."
So says Jacca Meneere about the summer visitors.

Well, I guess he had a pretty hard time with that lot who
came down last year. They blamed him for the disappearance
of the awful father. Not entirely fair, of course. You see, I
know what really happened.

They arrived late one Friday night in a posh four-by-four
having driven down that day from somewhere in the
Midlands. As soon as they began taking their luggage out of
the vehicle, the father started telling everyone, Jacca included,
that he knew all about the area and no-one could possibly
tell him anything new or interesting.

This irritating behaviour continued over the next few days
every time he encountered anyone at all, whether a resident
or a visitor. "Some hobnokshus," Jacca said. Others weren't
so polite.

Ginger beard stuck out at a ridiculous angle and waggling as
he spoke, or rather bellowed, the father continued to make
his presence felt at every opportunity. His amber eyes glowed
with conceit as he held forth on all things local. Certain that
'Ole Ginger Beard' didn't know everything about the area, a
plan was forming in Jacca's mind. Next Thursday it would
be full moon. And it was a blue moon too, when there are
two full moons in one month.

He stomped about the yard planning his tactics. Suddenly a

small hand was inserted into his. "Who is Ginger Beer, Grandad?" said a small voice.

"Not Ginger Beer, my boy," said Jacca. "Though they got a lot of things the same – full of fizz and pop and too much of it turns yer stomick! Just wait, my boy, and we'll see something very hinterestin' nex' week. Some fun will be had."

The days moved slowly on, with Ginger Beard becoming more unpleasant and full of himself as each one dawned. But Jacca had been observing the unpleasant visitor and being a good judge of human nature thought he had the measure of him. Finding himself alone with him in the yard he struck with the accuracy of a tropical snake.

"D'you knaw that you can git special powers by goin' up to they ole stones over yon' when the moon's up full?" Jacca asked Ginger Beard on Thursday morning, as he was preparing to go and collect his daily paper from the local shop.

As there was no-one else around, despite himself, the visitor showed some interest in what Jacca was saying. Any local knowledge that he could impart loudly, not only to his long-suffering family but any passing visitors, appealed to his vanity. He liked to know things that others did not.

"Do you mean the standing stones up on the moor?" he asked nonchalantly, and Jacca knew he had him!

"Why yes!" he replied. "On a blue moon, which 'appens to be tonight, you have to go up there alone and walk three times around the stones saying special words."

"Special words?" Ginger Beard questioned, trying not to show too much obvious interest.

"'Es. You got to say:

> Stone and water, air and earth,
> Altogether to give birth
> *Ro dhym Nerth* *
> By the moon and nightime dew
> May I be made a part of you.

And amazing powers will be yours."

Jacca's family had been the guardians of those stones above their farm for generation after generation; he knew all their secrets.

The day wore on and when darkness finally came Jacca and his grandson crouched behind the old stone hedge in the moonlight, making sure that they couldn't be seen from the narrow, uneven path that led to the ancient stones. After a short wait their patience was rewarded by the site of a stooped figure wearing an old coat and with an unmistakeable ginger beard protruding from its top. He glanced furtively from side to side making sure that he was completely alone.

Old Ginger Beard made his way uncertainly up the steep track towards the monument. He puffed and panted as he passed them in their hiding place and soon reached the flat area where the stones stood, illumined by the full moon. He was silhouetted against the night sky and they watched, fascinated, as he walked slowly widdershins around the stones saying out loud the words that Jacca had told him that morning.

After the third time the stones seemed to spin around and the man disappeared from view. When they stopped all that could be seen was their normal, familiar shapes in the moonlight. But where was Ginger Beard? Both boy and

*give me Power

man rushed to the top of the carn to see what had happened to him. He was nowhere to be seen.

Then Jacca lifted the young boy up so that he could look high up at the top part of the largest stone. What he saw made his blood run cold and he has never forgotten it – a pair of amber eyes looking pleadingly out from the stone. And this year people have remarked that there seems to be considerably more spiky orange lichen around the top of the largest standing stone.

An Dewhelans – The Return

To say that it had been a long journey from New South Wales to Penzance was a bit of an understatement; it had seemed interminable. But now, as I sat in the afternoon sun on the tiny patch of green called the Bowjey above Newlyn harbour, with St Michael's Mount shimmering in the haze across the bay, I knew it had definitely been worth the effort, tiredness and discomfort. My great-grandfather had been a fisherman, not here, but around the headland in Mousehole. It was my first visit to Kernow and I was captivated by its beauty and atmosphere. I could understand why it was a popular holiday destination for tourists from over the border. However, I felt as though I belonged and was not just a visitor from the other side of the globe. I am not a devout man, but at that moment it seemed right to ask St Michael for a blessing and his protection and guidance.

With the heat of the sun and the lunchtime pint of Hick's I began to feel drowsy. My head felt heavy so I gave myself up to the warmth and contentment of a Cornish afternoon … and I began to dream … and that dream changed my life. I'll try and tell you about it, as best as I can.

I saw a woman, old and yet still strikingly beautiful, standing on a rock and gazing out to sea; her hair windswept and her eyes wild. Her translucent skin glistened like pearl as though she had been underground and away from the light for many years. Her robe hung in folds around her thin body, braced against the wind. She slowly turned her face to me. She looked disconsolate and pale, but her eyes burned like molten tin, flashing and on the edge of madness – driven there by deep sorrow. But she was proud, and as I watched she recovered herself and seemed to grow in stature and stand more upright. She turned her body towards me and said:

An Spyrys a Gernow of vy. I am the Spirit of Cornwall. I am the soul of your native land. Listen to me now as I tell my story.

I am tired. Very tired. I am oppressed. I am bruised and torn. I have been raped and left for dead. I will not die while one person who loves me is left alive, but I am withering and becoming weak.

I have been loved. O, I have known such love! Love that would endure the fire and the anvil, the poison spear, the salt-sea drowning. And I know that there are those who love me still, but they are not strong enough alone, though they would give their very lives for me, to save and protect me. I ask that more of you will return to love me and cherish me. I need to be nurtured and protected by my own.

Listen with your heart as I speak from mine. I call to your soul from my soul. If ever I needed you it is now, O my people. I weep for myself and for our future. I beg you, do not neglect the land that gave you birth. I am your mother and father from whose granite and clay you were fashioned, whose rivers run in your veins, whose sea-water is your very blood. Your flesh is my flesh; your bone is my bone.

My language is the language of your heart.
My dance and music is your joy and laughter.
My vision is the vision of your inner eye.

What is happening to me now is far worse than anything I have endured over the centuries. It is subtle and hidden and more insidious. My very existence is threatened. I lie bleeding and broken. With the mining, I gave freely of my riches for the good of my children. They carved my body and dug into me with sharp tools. They burned and charred me. And still I gave like a generous mother. And they loved and honoured me as the giver – the bounteous one. Crofty, Geevor, Dolcoath – they are all gone now.

The granite that holds the land together is my bone. The soft green fields, my flesh. I am Tyrsans; I am the sacred land.

Listen! Can you hear the sound of the horn, *Corn a'n Wlas*, ringing out to alert all those Cornish around the earth that their country lies struggling and dying? Tell the world what is happening to me. You are my voice. Make known my plight – the abuse, the injustice. You can make a difference whether I live or die.

She paused, drew her cloak closer around her body, gave a shudder and continued. Do you remember what the Irish poet wrote about his native Ireland a century and a half ago?

"I dreamt that a lion lay bleeding in fetters,
Fast bound on an isle of the far Western wave ..."
It could have been written about me. But I don't see a lion; I see a slumbering black beast with red eyes and claws.

But what is this I spy through the silver mist?

Black bird of night
We call you home
The wild cliffs and dizzy ledges
Spray thrown up from stormy seas
Of green and grey
A quickening flash of red
Knife edge in air
Cut the mist with razor wing
Bird of night you will bring
A new day for our country

We have been given a sign of hope with the return of the chough to our shores. The bird which embodies the spirit of Arthur – the Once and Future King who will return when he is most needed. His spirit is returning to the people and the land. But he is only the forerunner, sent to summon you to come back to me. *Nyns yu marow Myghtern Arthur.* King Arthur is not dead. The time has come for him to return to Kernow. Will you come too?

You do not need to come to me in your body, for I know my children have been scattered to the four winds. You have made other lives for yourselves under hot suns and high mountains. On foreign shores where rich metals lie under the ground: where diamonds, silver and gold lie buried in the dark earth. Return to me in your spirit! Give me your allegiance.

Your ancestors were forced from the land by hunger and poverty. They did not want to leave me. You are not poor and starving. You have a choice – and I have no one but you to redeem me and make me live again. I am in need. Do not abandon me now. You are my heart and my hands. You are my only hope. Return to me, my children. *Dewheleugh dhym, fleghes vy!*

And then I saw a parade of people in the distance – men, women and children following a black beast and with a chough flying and swooping above its head. The beast carried a flag bearing a white cross on a black ground – Baner Peran – over its shoulder as it strode forth, head erect, teeth bared, leading the procession.

The woman, waiting on the shore to welcome home her family, threw her arms open wide, embracing them as they came ashore from the sea and as they streamed down from the hills behind her. Her radiance spread a light that reflected from their faces, some wet with tears of joy. They came in their tens, and then in their hundreds and thousands, smiling and laughing, glad to be home. *Aga Mamvro*. Their homeland.

I awoke to the sound of the gulls screaming over the harbour below and this message echoing in my ears:

You are my only hope. Return to me, my children. *Dewheleugh dhym, fleghes vy!*

And I knew what I had to do.